DOERS

21

Just Your Handyman

Kurt Armstrong

Some people build skyscrapers. I address that damp spot on your kitchen ceiling.

ESSAY

26

To Mend a Farm

Adam Nicolson

A restored landscape will be more than it was before, bearing the marks of damage and repair.

REPORT

46

The Home You Carry with You

Stephanie Saldaña

A church that prays in the language of Jesus, scattered by war, lives on in many new places.

REFLECTION

60

Heaven Meets Earth

Rowan Williams

In the birth of Christ, God comes to restore and set free every person and all creation.

PORTFOLIO

64

Face to Face

Hannah Rose Thomas

Art gives a voice to women who have survived violence in forgotten corners of the world.

STORY

106

Hunger

Narine Abgaryan

In this story set in 1990s Armenia, survivors of war find a reason to go on living.

Plough

INSIGHTS

ESSAY

11 **Three Pillars of Education**

Children flourish when home, school, and community align.

Heinrich Arnold

EDITORIAL

15 **In Praise of Repair Culture**

Modern life depends on the habit of discarding things. What if we fixed them instead?

Peter Mommsen

DOERS

32 **Visible Repair**

A mom makes mended clothes beautiful.

Leah Libresco Sargeant

ESSAY

36 **Empty Pews**

A young minister in a declining church looks for reasons to hope.

Benjamin Crosby

INTERVIEW

56 **Culture Care and Repair**

The creative arts are about imagining the future as it could be.

Makoto Fujimura

READINGS

78 **Forgiveness**

Four writers reflect on the restorative power of personal forgiveness.

Catherine de Hueck Doherty, Teresa of Ávila, Desmond Tutu, and Jacques Philippe

PERSONAL HISTORY

83 **If Prisons Could Rehabilitate**

Perhaps some things can't be repaired, but that doesn't mean we shouldn't try.

Carlo Gébler

ESSAY

98 **Architecture for Humans**

Can people live in hope if their homes and places of work do not nurture and celebrate life?

Norman Wirzba

READING

112 **Yielding to God**

The Christ Child is born in the poverty of our hearts.

Philip Britts

ARTS & LETTERS

REVIEWS

53 **What We're Reading**

Elizabeth Genovise on *Holler*, Elizabeth Wainwright on *The Quickening*, and Amy Parilee Rickards on *Remarkably Bright Creatures*.

ESSAY

90 **Ifs Eternally**

Maybe we don't have to figure it all out.

Christian Wiman

POETRY

31 **Andy Mayhew**

45 **Daedalus**

Amit Majmudar

DEPARTMENTS

LETTERS

4 Readers Respond

FAMILY AND FRIENDS

7 Education in Prison
Sean Sword

One Parish, One Prisoner
Chris Hoke

Building a Culture of Repair
Alan Koppschall

COMMUNITY SNAPSHOT

87 Analog Hero
One man's quest to fix the world,
one toaster at a time.
Maureen Swinger

FORERUNNERS

120 The Sweet Power of Green Vigor
Hildegard of Bingen sought to
express "the sacred sound through
which all creation resounds."
Susannah Black Roberts

WEB EXCLUSIVES

Read these articles at *plough.com/web38*

REVIEW

Who Can Repair the World?
Tikkun olam in the novels of
Eugene Vodolazkin.
Nadya Williams

REPORT

Rebuilding Notre-Dame Cathedral
It's not the first time it has
risen from the ashes.
Elizabeth Lev

INTERVIEW

Could I Do That?
A novelist grapples with
undeserved forgiveness.
Em Strang

Plough

ANOTHER LIFE IS POSSIBLE

EDITOR: Peter Mommsen
SENIOR EDITORS: Shana Goodwin, Maria Hine,
Maureen Swinger, Sam Hine, Susannah Black Roberts
EDITOR-AT-LARGE: Caitrin Keiper
BOOKS AND CULTURE EDITOR: Joy Marie Clarkson
POETRY EDITOR: A. M. Juster
DESIGNERS: Rosalind Stevenson, Miriam Burleson
CREATIVE DIRECTOR: Clare Stober
COPY EDITORS: Wilma Mommsen, Priscilla Jensen
FACT CHECKER: Suzanne Quinta
MARKETING DIRECTOR: Trevor Wiser
UK EDITION: Ian Barth
CONTRIBUTING EDITORS: Leah Libresco Sargeant,
Brandon McGinley, Jake Meador, Madoc Cairns
FOUNDING EDITOR: Eberhard Arnold (1883–1935)
Plough Quarterly No. 38: Repair
Published by Plough Publishing House, ISBN 978-1-63608-130-4
Copyright © 2024 by Plough Publishing House. All rights reserved.

EDITORIAL OFFICE
151 Bowne Drive
Walden, NY 12586
T: 845.572.3455
info@plough.com

SUBSCRIBER SERVICES
PO Box 8542
Big Sandy, TX 75755
T: 800.521.8011
subscriptions@plough.com

United Kingdom
Brightling Road
Robertsbridge
TN32 5DR
T: +44(0)1580.883.344

Australia
4188 Gwydir Highway
Elsmore, NSW
2360 Australia
T: +61(0)2.6723.2213

Plough Quarterly (ISSN 2372-2584) is published quarterly by
Plough Publishing House, PO Box 398, Walden, NY 12586.
Individual subscription $36 / £24 / €28 per year.
Subscribers outside of the United States and Canada pay in British pounds or euros.
Periodicals postage paid at Walden, NY 12586 and at additional mailing offices.
POSTMASTER: Send address changes to Plough Quarterly, PO Box 8542, Big Sandy, TX 75755.

Front cover: *Darning Sampler (Germany)*, Wikimedia Commons (public domain).
Inside front cover: Joseph Zbukvic, *Boat Repairs*, watercolor, 2010. Used by permission.
Back cover: J. Kirk Richards, *Mother and Child*, oil, 2001. Used by permission.
Back cover text trans. K. E. Roberts.

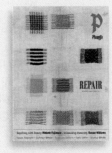

ABOUT THE COVER

The work of repair, in its variety
of manifestations, is gracefully
rendered in this carefully stitched
darning sampler from nineteenth-
century Germany. Whether simple
or complex, the stitches weave
together to reinforce worn cloth and
give it more life.

LETTERS

Readers respond to *Plough*'s Issue 37, *The Enemy*. Send letters to *letters@plough.com*.

THE CHANGE WE NEED

Very recently I came across a phrase (probably in *Plough*!) that struck me as "just right" for describing the changes so many of us need to make if life on our planet has any chance of continuing: "downward mobility." That's another way of framing time-honored spiritual advice to simplify, freeing ourselves from stuff. Our social aspirations have (always?) been upward mobility whenever possible. A big divergence.

What we need now – must bring about – is a cultural and spiritual transformation, away from greed, selfishness, and indifference. However, in my experience otherwise decent, civically minded, church-going humans can react angrily to the idea of reducing their conveniences.

I would greatly appreciate *Plough* digging into this topic – if you haven't already – specifically in the "environmental" sense. Bearing in mind, also, that

there's a growing conviction (which I share) that we need to reappraise our notions of human supremacy.

Kristine Montamat, Charlottesville, Virginia

SAYING NO TO WAR

On Rachel Cañon Naffziger's "A Russian Christian Speaks Out": I read with interest two articles in your latest issue, one on the Russian pacifist and the other on Jesus' call to love our enemies. Reading the latter, one could easily argue today that Jesus is calling us Christians in the West to love the Russians, instead of sending billions of dollars' worth of weapons to Ukraine to kill them. When *Plough* published an article a while back about a Ukrainian priest, formerly a pacifist and now supporting the Ukrainian military, the article suggested no disagreement with the priest, with only obvious support for his good work in a war zone. (Of course, I have no argument with the fact he is doing good things.) Now, regarding Egor Redin, the Russian pacifist, I also have no disagreement with his brave stance. Perhaps you could also profile a Ukrainian pacifist who has been recently arrested for his pacifist stance. For example, there is Yurii Sheliazhenko, now under house arrest, who is part of the World Beyond War international organization as well as a Ukrainian pacifist organization.

But is it not time to make it clear that *Plough* does not support the arming of Ukraine to continue this insane war? I am more than a little dismayed by the lack of a strong stance on this issue, especially given the potential for escalation to nuclear annihilation that we face today. Some readers might wonder whether *Plough*, like so many today, might be watering down its

pacifist stance because of the Ukraine war. Knowing you, I find it hard to believe this would be the case, but others might not.

Jim Dowling, Brisbane, Australia

Editors: Plough has never supported the arming of warring parties. That has not changed.

DID JESUS HAVE ENEMIES?

On T. J. Keiderling's "Tough Love on the Mount": Your conclusion that it is "power figures" that are the "enemies" and often the most difficult to love is very pertinent. I would like to pick up on two points: First, your article might be read to suggest that Pharisees were not Jesus' enemies. However, in the story of the man with the shriveled hand (Matt. 12:14, Mark 3:6, Luke 6:11) those referred to as Pharisees clearly plot to kill Jesus. There is definite enmity from Pharisees on that occasion, as well as in other cases.

Second, in your article you examine various groups of people: Pharisees, Sadducees, Romans, tax collectors, and those in power, pondering whether they are Jesus' enemies. In fact, Jesus answered the question himself: "Whoever is not with me is against me" (Matt. 12:30, Luke 11:23). Jesus does not align or oppose himself to our human sects, our nationalities, or our socioeconomic or political categories. Rather, he asks, are we with him, or not? Do we work to gather into his kingdom or scatter?

By this definition, each of us can, and sometimes does, become an enemy of Jesus. It is in that recognition we can truly understand his command to love our enemies.

Francis Köppschall, Dover, United Kingdom

DIFFICULT FORGIVENESS

On Benjamin Crosby's "Foolhardy Wisdom": It's just over a year since I was canceled, threatened with trespass charges should I ever again appear on the property of the church on whose council I served. The only time someone from that church has checked in on me since was a quick question from the head of prayer ministry after we'd seen each other maybe thirty weeks in a row at a club we both belong to. Thanks for the timely reminder of my responsibility to fulfill the very difficult and costly task of forgiveness.

Carlene Hill Byron, Topsham, Maine

WHEN OUR MINDS ARE AGAINST US

On Sarah Clarkson's "My Mind, My Enemy": I have one adult child who has OCD and one with bipolar disorder. Both are incredible human beings but they are learning to steward the package God has given them. How do any of us embrace the awfulness and the awesomeness of who God has made us to be? But as Sarah Clarkson so beautifully conveys, there is beauty in brokenness and Jesus is the only one who can show us how to hold both and experience redemption.

Debbie Childers, Greensboro, North Carolina

LOVING OR HATING SINNERS

On Mary Townsend's "Hating Sinners": I have had a longtime interest in the easy hiding place that is the cliché, "Love the sinner, hate the sin." I gained much from your words. I fear, though, that there was much I missed; parts were too esoteric for me. I am not an academic and wonder how much more enlightening it would have been – especially to many who so easily slip behind the "hate the sin" veil – if written in plainer language. I am not suggesting dumbing down your argument, but what if it had been written more as one might write a sermon, or at least with such a diverse audience in mind?

John Hart Marshall Hull, Harrisonburg, Virginia

FRUITFUL DEBATE

On Leah Libresco Sargeant's "Students Brave the Heat": I appreciated reading this detailed account of educational courage. Having been a high school English teacher for several years, I understand how challenging it can be to cultivate a classroom environment that is curious and amicable rather than adversarial. I feel especially moved by those students who come into a lesson already "armed for conflict," often for complex reasons outside their control.

I think of one boy I began teaching when he was fourteen. He had been out of education for over a year when he arrived, and became homeless more than once during his two years in my class. We got off to a rocky start: his insecurities expressed themselves as apathy and defiance, mine as aloofness and roboticism. But a turning point came during a lesson on Tennyson's "The Charge of the Light Brigade." After a bit of military history, I did a couple of tricks with a plastic sword to illustrate the "sabers" in the poem. At the

About Us

Plough is published by the Bruderhof, an international community of families and singles seeking to follow Jesus together. Members of the Bruderhof are committed to a way of radical discipleship in the spirit of the Sermon on the Mount. Inspired by the first church in Jerusalem (Acts 2 and 4), they renounce private property and share everything in common in a life of nonviolence, justice, and service to neighbors near and far. There are twenty-nine Bruderhof settlements in both rural and urban locations in the United States, England, Germany, Australia, Paraguay, South Korea, and Austria, with around 3000 people in all. To learn more or arrange a visit, see the community's website at *bruderhof.com*.

Plough features original stories, ideas, and culture to inspire faith and action. Starting from the conviction that the teachings and example of Jesus can transform and renew our world, we aim to apply them to all aspects of life, seeking common ground with all people of goodwill regardless of creed. The goal of *Plough* is to build a living network of readers, contributors, and practitioners so that, as we read in Hebrews, we may "spur one another on toward love and good deeds."

Plough includes contributions that we believe are worthy of our readers' consideration, whether or not we fully agree with them. Views expressed by contributors are their own and do not necessarily reflect the editorial position of *Plough* or of the Bruderhof communities.

end I heard a quiet, "Sir – can you show me how to do that?" What an opportunity! I did, of course.

After that, I found I no longer had to go into those lessons praying for grace to love my enemy. That moment of curiosity and vulnerability (especially on my student's part – the teacher was doing something worth imitating?!) turned us into educational allies. Of course, it wasn't all straightforward from there, but we were no longer at loggerheads. Instead we stood, as we had with our plastic swords, shoulder to shoulder.

Dominic Palmer, Manchester, United Kingdom

LIVING OUT THE TRUTH

On Dana Wiser's "Macedonia Morning": This article captures the essence of who my father was and of my parents' life together with more insight than any other "obituary" I have read. It also helps me understand my family heritage more fully. The only

change that I would have suggested is the definition of my father as a self-styled existentialist. The emphasis certainly would be more on "self-styled." As my mother told me, he considered himself to be a Marxist Quaker. I think he had a longing for truth that is closer to religion than the philosophy of an existentialist. And he had tremendous concern for how that truth was lived out in human relationships, "love of neighbor" lived out in the personal, communal, political, and economic spheres.

Barbara Lynd Bond, Warren, Ohio

The social gospel emphasis of the Lynds was the worldview I grew up on among liberal Quakers. Although I have spent my entire professional career engaged in quintessential social gospel work as a public defender and have had the opportunity to speak into many lives, I am absolutely convinced that the real power is not in the social gospel but in the actual gospel – the witness, ministry, sacrificial death, and bodily resurrection of Jesus Christ. As we have seen in communist/Marxist movements, there is this impulse to coerce, threaten, imprison, or kill those who stand in the way of the "progressive" cause of the day, whereas the gospel of Jesus Christ teaches that change comes one heart at a time as we learn, with the help of the power of the Holy Spirit, to die to ourselves and live for Christ. We would rather suffer ourselves than force others to accept our truths.

Thomas N. N. Angell, Clinton Corners, New York

STATEMENT OF OWNERSHIP, MANAGEMENT, AND CIRCULATION
(Required by 39 U.S.C. 3685)
Title of publication: Plough Quarterly. Publication No: 0001-6584. 3. Date of filing: October 1, 2023. 4. Frequency of issue: Quarterly. 5. Number of issues published annually: 4. 6. Annual subscription price: $36.00. 7. Complete mailing address of known office of publication: Plough Quarterly, P.O. Box 398, Walden, NY 12586. 8. Same. 9. Publisher: Plough Publishing House, same address. Editor: Peter Mommsen, same address. Managing Editor: Sam Hine, same address. 10. Owner: Plough Publishing House, P.O. Box 398, Walden, NY 12586. 11. Known bondholders, mortgages, and other securities: None. 12. The purpose, function, and nonprofit status of this organization and the exempt status for federal income tax purposes have not changed during preceding 12 months. 13. Publication Title: Plough Quarterly. 14. Issue date for circulation data below: Fall 2022–Summer 2023. 15. Extent and nature of circulation: Average No. copies of each issue during preceding 12 months: A. Total number of copies (net press run): 16,875. B.1. Mailed outside-county paid subscriptions: 13,464. B.2. Mailed in-county paid subscriptions: 0. B.3. Paid distribution outside the mails including sales through dealers and carriers, street vendors, counter sales, and other non-USPS paid distribution: 325. B.4. Other classes mailed through the USPS: 0. C. Total paid distribution: 13,789. D.1. Free distribution by mail: Outside-county: 1,239. D.2. In-county: 0. D.3. Other classes mailed through the USPS: 0. Free distribution outside the mail: 43. E. Total free distribution: 1,282. F. Total Distribution: 15,070. G. Copies not distributed: 1,805. H. Total: 16,875. I. Percent paid: 91.49%. Actual No. copies of single issue published nearest to filing date: A.: 17,500. B.1.: 14,314. B.2.: 0. B.3.: 318. B.4.: 0. C.: 14,632. D.1.: 1,265. D.2.: 0. D.3.: 0. D.4.: 42. E.: 1,307. F.: 15,939. G.: 1,561. H.: 17,500. I.: 91.80 %. Electronic copy circulation: Average No. copies of each issue during preceding 12 months: A. Total No. Electronic Copies: 52. B. Total paid print copies plus paid electronic copies: 13,840. C. Total print distribution plus paid electronic copies: 15,122. D. Percent paid: 91.52%. Actual No. copies of single issue published nearest to filing date: A.: 43. B.: 14,675. C.: 15,982. D.: 91.82%. 17. Publication of Statement of Ownership: Winter 2024. 18. I certify that the statements made by me above are correct and complete. Sam Hine, Editor, September 15, 2023.

FAMILY & FRIENDS

AROUND THE WORLD

Education in Prison

Practicing the liberal arts exposed me to topics such as truth, the good life, and justice, and restored my trust in humanity.

Sean Sword

Who has time for conversing about old books and abstract ideas such as truth, the good life, or justice? One clear answer to this question would be: individuals confined in prison seeking a path toward rehabilitation, as well as corrections officials who want to protect the public while simultaneously providing prisoners with an opportunity for growth.

The confines of prison compel individuals who seek a path of rehabilitation to engage in a soul-searching process and reflect on various aspects of a life gone astray. Most of that reflection is done in isolation or solitude where human qualities such as kindness, civility, and love are absent. Because we are relational beings, those missing qualities severely restrict a proper reception of any type of education. When the Michigan Department of Corrections allowed the opportunity for prisoners to participate in a faith-based education, the liberal arts were liberated – freed from their confinement to schools, they broke through prison walls.

This liberal arts program has created a space for kindness, civility, and love to flourish at the Richard A. Handlon campus in Ionia, Michigan. Students and staff have become better-integrated human beings as a result, and although rehabilitation does not happen in an instant, the liberal arts play a key role in the prisoner's restoration to society.

Through the generosity of donors who wish to participate in the restorative process, Calvin University and Calvin Theological Seminary provided me with training in the liberal arts while I was in prison. This experience enhanced my ability to apply discussions of truth, the good life, and justice to my life in two ways. First, it provided me with a path to redemption and

Sean Sword is a student majoring in criminology at Calvin University. A juvenile offender, he served twenty-seven years in prison, and while there he began his college studies through the Calvin Prison Initiative. This excerpt is taken from The Liberating Arts *(Plough, 2023).*

reconciliation through the teachings of Christ, which gave balance and clarity in a spiritual sense. Second, I was attracted to the idea of servant leadership, geared toward restoration of my relationship with society and starting with staff and prisoners within the facility. Together, these two aspects served as a much-needed balm for the shame of past wrongs and a solid foundation for returning to life as a citizen in society.

Guiding me toward a vocation and a vision of God's kingdom, the faith-based component of my education has been instrumental, since it is most responsible for my relationship with professors, staff, and other students. These relationships are about more than just the exchange of information; they are about inquiry into truth, the good life, justice, and love in relation to others – reflecting the character of Christ and the relational qualities most yearned for in the prison setting.

This educational ministry carries over into the overwhelming expression of support that I have received since being released from prison and continuing my studies on Calvin's main campus at Knollcrest. Students and faculty have welcomed me with open arms. I attend classes and campus events brimming with confidence that I have a home within this community. My trust in humanity has been restored, and the process of reconciliation with God and his creation is my top priority.

Another major influence in restoring my trust in humanity has been the liberal arts curriculum and the vibrant learning environment it produces at the university. It is a mirror image of what was happening at the Handlon campus where I started my courses and embarked on a serious effort at being able to trust again. Communication between prisoners, officers, and administration improved dramatically. Calvin Prison Initiative students began to engage the larger prison population as peer-to-peer mentors, tutors for the various vocational trade programs, and effective mediators who prevented violence within the facility.

At the Knollcrest campus, the liberal arts forum allows for students and faculty to become better educated about the criminal justice system and the lives of those within its grasp. I don't know of many educational opportunities where a twenty-year-old college student who wants to be a lawyer has a classmate who served twenty-seven years in prison. Imagine the rich content that is found in a sociology class focused on corrections and incarceration, or a statistics and probability course that studies the mean, median, and mode of incarceration numbers at all levels of government. That is what the liberal arts provides: an opportunity to learn from each other based on life experiences, academic instruction, and direction toward vocation in society.

The prisoners and staff who make up the population of a prison are a microcosm of what is found in the larger societies we live in. I was sentenced to life without parole at the age of seventeen for crimes against society. The liberal arts have exposed me to topics such as truth, the good life, and justice and allowed me to restore my relationship with God and his creation in a way that has changed my life forever.

One Parish, One Prisoner

Underground Ministries is pioneering a program that matches former inmates with local churches for ongoing support and friendship.

Chris Hoke

When Adrian Cavala signed up for our new One Parish One Prisoner reentry program at Underground Ministries here in Washington State, he sent me a private prison email. He had his doubts.

I'd known him on the streets over my last decade of pastoral work among gang members in our rural Skagit Valley. We'd gotten to know each other better when squeezed into a small utility closet at a distant prison, when the guards didn't have a chapel room for our visits. Adrian, known on the streets as "Spade," could imagine trusting a full-time gang chaplain like me, but not "normies": regular folks, mostly white, from the large evangelical church in town who'd signed up to become his One Parish One Prisoner reentry team. They didn't know a thing about the underground world of meth, crime, and survival bonds. Even though it was the same town, they were separate worlds.

"Honestly, I've felt that once they get to know me they may not like me," he wrote in this email. "But then I remember how much many of us in prison have in common, even though we come from different backgrounds. Even the hardest homies I have ever met while doing time seem so unapproachable and uninviting. But once I get to know them and actually see them, we would end up having great relationships. We would be laughing all the time and clowning around."

Without even a paragraph break, he pivoted: "I'm gonna put the same kind of outlook towards the people of the church as well. I mean, i'm a freakin' delight, lol! So, they too might end up being some freakin' delights in my life."

This is the hidden treasure of prison reentry work, for us. Not just helping men and women being released from prison get some resources, a job, and – in the dismally utilitarian phrase – become "productive members of society." Rather, we see what freakin' delights they are, beneath the mummy-wrapping of their addictions or learned violence. And, in the gift of their trust and raw authenticity, we on the outside might discover what freakin' delights we are, as well – beneath our "normie" veneers as productive members of society.

Over the following months, as the team followed our twenty-four monthly learning modules, they wrote letters to Adrian. They made the long drive to the prison, entered the razor-wire fortress, and learned from him about how he and his celly made a "prison tamale" out of Doritos and a spicy pickle from the commissary snacks. They built a comprehensive reentry plan with him. The church prayed for Adrian, heard his letters read from the platform. A woman on the team sent Adrian photos of her growing tomato garden, and soon they were swapping stories about family tamale recipes.

Turns out members of the church had sons and daughters struggling with addiction.

Chris Hoke is the author of Wanted *(HarperOne, 2015) and executive director of Underground Ministries. UndergroundMinistries.org.*

They didn't really talk about it, and so suffered alone. With Adrian now, a new space of tenderness was opening between them. New honesty for grief and growth was weaving their worlds.

Adrian was released last month, and I got a text message from a new number: "Sup Chris, check out me and my team". A batch of photos buzzed in: he and seven folks I didn't know were lined up at the Skagit River, grilling the coho salmon they'd pulled out of the August waters together.

In another text message, Adrian wrote me last month: "I thank God all the time for putting people that genuinely care in my life. So even though I fear to fail and I fear to let people down – I will try again – and again and again. This time though, I'm not doing it alone."

Building a Culture of Repair

A repair café is a neighborhood meeting place where you can repair your things with the help of volunteers.

Alan Koppschall

The basement of St. Peter's Lutheran Church in Port Jervis, New York, is lit with bright fluorescent lights. Clothes are piled high on tables pushed against the walls. In winter, the space is used as a warming station: a place where people without homes can find a hot meal and a warm place to stay. No one is coming here for warmth today – it's 85 degrees Fahrenheit outside – but a sign by the door explains in large lettering made with blue masking tape: REPAIR CAFE, 1–4 P.M. TODAY! FREE!

I'm carrying an espresso machine that belongs to friends (bougie, I know). The steam wand doesn't work, and I'm hoping someone can fix it.

The repair café movement arrived in New York's Hudson Valley in 2013. Since then, volunteers have started over fifty such "cafés" in the area. The concept is simple: people bring a broken household item – garden clippers, a chair, kitchen knives, a lamp, even jewelry – to a neighborhood location, and volunteers try to fix it for them. If a spare part is needed, the item's owner will purchase it, but the labor is free.

Only four years before the first repair café opened in New York State, Dutch journalist and environmentalist Martine Postma founded the world's first in Amsterdam. Distressed by "throwaway culture," in which businesses design products with intentionally short lifespans, she realized that many

Minutes after his release from prison, a One Parish One Prisoner participant embraces his father in the prison parking lot.

Winter 2024 9

people had lost the skills of repair. To rebuild a repair culture, Postma gathered her fellow fixers and invited Amsterdam residents to bring their broken items. "A repair café is a neighborhood meeting place where you, with help from skillful volunteers, can repair your things," she told journalists. "It's fun: you meet people from the neighborhood and you also help the environment." The movement grew quickly to 2,500 repair cafés worldwide.

Pete Marchetto and his wife, Katie, run the Port Jervis repair café. Pete fixes electrical and mechanical items and Katie patches jeans, mends quilts, and repairs other textile items. In a back corner, Wesley, a professional handyman, cuts a broken slat off a wooden chair with an oscillating saw. Seated at a table near the middle of the space, another volunteer sharpens kitchen knives and garden tools.

"I've never fixed one of these before," Pete tells me when he sees the espresso machine I'm carrying, "but I'll see what I can do." He plugs it into the wall. It makes a hissing noise as it starts to heat up.

Pete and Katie have been fixing things for years. They were graduate students when their washing machine broke down. Pete remembers: "We get the repair guy to come out and take a look at it. He tells us that the circuit board needs replacing, which would cost around $300 for the part and $200 for the labor. I ask him if I can take a look, as my background is in electronics. I take the cover off and see that there is one little chip with a tiny divot in the top of it. I find the exact chip online to replace it: it's 68 cents. Two minutes of soldering work, and we have a working washing machine." Since then, Pete and Katie have tried to repair their broken items rather than throw them out. When they heard about the repair cafés, they organized one.

"We like to see ourselves as repair coaches," Pete tells me as he adjusts the knobs on the espresso machine. "As much as we're fixing people's broken stuff, we're also teaching them how to repair it the next time it breaks." He points over at Wesley, who is explaining the bonding properties of different kinds of wood glue to the woman who owns the chair he's fixing. While we are talking, Pete has turned on the steam wand. It seems to work again. He explains to me that possibly a piece of limescale, stuck in its silicone tubing, worked itself loose on the drive down. "Sometimes, you just look at a broken item and it repairs itself," he says with a smile.

As a Port Jervis local, Pete feels a responsibility to his hometown, one of the poorest in New York. This motivated him and Katie to found the repair café. By offering to repair broken items for free, they hoped to build a culture of repair among their neighbors. They tell me that repair shop owners in other towns, rather than dreading the arrival of a free repair café or fearing the loss of business, welcomed them. Once people learn that a broken item can be fixed, they are much less likely to throw it out and buy a new one.

Pete and Katie see their small acts of repair as part of the task of Christians to help renew a broken world. "Christ takes our brokenness and our sin and restores us because of his love for us. As Christians, we are called to imitate Christ. If we can't repair the brokenness of the world, at least we can repair our neighbor's grass clippers, his chair, or his lamp."

Poet In This Issue:

Amit Majmudar served as Ohio's first poet laureate and works as a diagnostic radiologist in Westerville, Ohio, where he lives with his wife and three children. His most recent books to be published in the United States are *Black Avatar: and Other Essays* (Acre Books, 2023) and *Twin A: A Memoir* (Slant Books, 2023). In addition, Penguin India published *The Book of Vows,* the first of three volumes in a Mahabharata retelling, as well as an original mythological story cycle, *The Later Adventures of Hanuman* (2023). Read his poems "Andy Mayhew" on page 31 and "Daedalus" on page 45.

Alan Koppschall is Plough's *events coordinator and a member of the Bruderhof. He lives at the Fox Hill Bruderhof in Walden, New York.*

Wesley mends a chair at the repair café in Port Jervis, New York.

Three Pillars of Education

In the Bruderhof, as in any society, we see how children flourish when family, school, and community align.

HEINRICH ARNOLD

CHILDREN ARE SPECIAL. They speak a universal language of joy, wonder, inquisitiveness, mischief, and love. They respond to a mother's nurture and a father's loving firmness. They have a natural hunger for learning and an instinct for truth, and flourish when they know they have a place in a community.

Education is the process of preparing children to inherit this world and make it better. It means guiding, equipping, teaching, and liberating the next generation. As a pastor in the Bruderhof community, as well as a father, grandfather, and former teacher, I see three essential pillars of education: family, school, and community. When

Pilar López Báez, *Raul*, mixed media on wood panel, 2017.

these three pillars work in harmony of purpose, they are like a three-legged stool that is stable even on uneven ground.

Faith is the foundation on which the three pillars stand or fall. Faith answers the important questions of purpose, direction, and hope, and can sustain families, schools, and communities. I think it is a mistake to divorce or isolate faith from education. In fact, I'd argue that faith and education are inseparable. Education seeks after truth – and not just any truth, but the certain, ultimate, and absolute truth that faith affirms. Abandoning truth leads to doubt, confusion, unhappiness, and division. On the other hand, faith in God's good and natural order leads to security and confidence. The late Rabbi Jonathan Sacks writes:

> One reason religion has survived in the modern world despite four centuries of secularization is that it answers the three questions every reflective human being will ask at some time in his or her life: Who am I? Why am I here? How then shall I live? These cannot be answered by the four great institutions of the modern West: science, technology, the market economy, and the liberal democratic state. Science tells us how but not why. Technology gives us power but cannot tell us how to use that power. The market gives us choices but does not tell us which choices to make. The liberal democratic state as a matter of principle holds back from endorsing any particular way of life. The result is that contemporary culture sets before us an almost infinite range of possibilities, but does not tell us who we are, why we are here, and how we should live.

If modern secular society has failed to answer these fundamental questions, we should welcome the presence of faith in our homes, schools, and communities. This is possible even in a pluralistic society – all the world's great religions, while not alike, do teach respect and the dignity of human life and offer answers to the important questions.

1. FAMILY

Family is the first pillar of education. A married mother and father forming a loving and stable family is undeniably the best arrangement in which to conceive, bear, and raise children. Many studies have confirmed this fact, which religions have taught for centuries. My Christian faith teaches faithfulness in marriage between one man and one woman; many other faiths teach this as well.

My mother and father modeled such a loving family and home. They married, raised eight children, and remained together for fifty-one years until their deaths at home, each surrounded by their sons, daughters, and grandchildren. My wife, Wilma, and I have seven wonderful children, three of whom have married. We have five grandchildren and hope for more!

My church, the Bruderhof, places high importance on the sacredness of marriage and prepares couples seeking to be married with rigorous counseling and teaching about the importance of faithfulness and commitment to each other through all difficulties of life. Commitment is vital to give children a chance to thrive. We have a model of this covenant of faithfulness in the biblical account of God's faithfulness to humankind throughout the millennia. Faithfulness still works, it is still beautiful, and it is still the surest precondition for bringing children into this world and raising them well. Every child deserves both a father and a mother living peacefully together to provide love, stability, and security. That said, I believe Jesus cares especially for children who don't grow up in such a home, and that he gives single parents the strength to do their best with their situation.

Heinrich Arnold serves as a senior pastor for the Bruderhof in the United States and abroad. He lives with his wife and family at the Woodcrest Bruderhof.

2. SCHOOLS

Schools are the second pillar of a child's education. Caring and dedicated teachers who are passionate about educating and forming children make a good school. Buildings and facilities are wonderful assets but never replace the teacher and a positive environment for learning.

Increasingly, parents are opting to homeschool, for reasons I respect deeply. But more often than not, the main reason is the failure of schools to provide a safe, wholesome space for socialization and qualified instruction, things most parents cannot be expected to provide on their own.

The Bruderhof runs schools from early childhood through high school. Our approach to education emphasizes connection with God's creation; thorough learning of math, science, writing, and communication; and an appreciation of history, literature, art, music, and crafts. The "head, heart, and hands" philosophy we've adopted stresses educating the whole child, bringing together the intellectual, emotional, and physical to train responsible, compassionate, and serving members of society. My grandmother Annemarie Wächter brought to our community the educational vision of her great-granduncle Friedrich Froebel, who invented the kindergarten. His early childhood pedagogy promotes learning through play and exploration of nature. Froebel said, "A child who plays thoroughly and perseveringly . . . will be a determined adult, capable of self-sacrifice both for his own welfare and that of others."

Pilar López Báez, *Escenas Familiares III*, acrylic on canvas, 2011.

3. COMMUNITY

Community is the final pillar of education, giving support, stability, and identity to families and individuals. Community can help fill some of the gaps that inevitably occur in children's lives when families struggle due to separation, difficult economic or domestic circumstances, and tragedies.

In my community, the Bruderhof, we make a lifetime commitment to one another. We find common ground and common cause in following the teachings of Jesus to forgive unconditionally,

---

Strong communities make strong families and strong children.

---

to renounce all violence, to live free from wealth, to serve as the least and lowest, and to give up power over others. We are a fellowship of brothers and sisters, both single and married, who are called by Christ to follow him together

in a common life like that of the first church in Jerusalem described in Acts 2 and 4.

Of course, not everyone finds themselves in a community as structured and supportive as the Bruderhof. But anyone can build community. Children love getting together to celebrate joyous milestones in life: births, birthdays, graduations, baptisms, marriages, anniversaries, and holidays. We all make up community: neighbors, friends from school and work, playgroups, youth groups, dad groups, mom groups, cultural or recreational clubs, sports teams, and faith communities. Strong communities make strong families and strong children. The Indian poet Rabindranath Tagore writes: "Children are living beings – more living than adults, who have built shells of habit around themselves. Therefore it is absolutely necessary for their mental health and development that they should have not only schools for their lessons, but a world whose guiding spirit is personal love."

Community is not government. The role of government should be to provide support services, structural stability, and rule of law in all public spheres of life, including education. It should protect and respect the role of faith in public life, without impinging on freedom of religion.

Education is the great passing on of the torch from one generation to the next. Strong families, schools, and communities make this possible. Faith is not a separate and cloistered part of life; it informs, vitalizes, and shapes education. Where such education exists, we can have great hope for the future, and joy in each child born into this world. As Tagore writes, "Every child comes with the message that God is not yet discouraged of man." ⤳

Pilar López Báez, *La Carrera*, mixed media on wood, 2015.

Artwork by Joseph Zbukvic. Used by permission.

In Praise of Repair Culture

Modern life depends on the habit of discarding things.
What if we fixed them instead?

PETER MOMMSEN

DO FARMERS HAVE A RIGHT to repair their own tractors? The American Farm Bureau Federation thinks so. That's why this year it reached an agreement with John Deere in which the manufacturer promised to enable farmers, as well as third-party mechanics, to fix their own green-and-yellow machinery,

for example by providing service manuals and diagnostic tools that earlier only licensed shops could access. For many farmers, this change could be economically transformative, enabling older tractors to be used longer rather than being replaced because of the high repair costs. The farmers' federation is now working to reach

Joseph Zbukvic, *Boat Repair*, watercolor on paper.

Joseph Zbukvic, *Fishing Boats,* watercolor on paper

similar agreements with other manufacturers.

The John Deere agreement is one more small but significant victory for the right to repair movement, which has been taking aim at practices in industries ranging from automotive to consumer electronics that restrict the ability to fix things, driving up costs for users and (often deliberately) forcing them to replace items that might still work. Targets include nonreplaceable laptop batteries, software updates that disable video game consoles, and toner cartridges programmed to stop printing even when they still contain ink.

In view of the role that discarded products play in clogging landfills and polluting drinking water, the movement argues that repair is key to addressing environmental damage from consumer capitalism. "You can't make them last if you can't make them work," one advocate told *Wirecutter.*

"Any time a manufacturer says that they are being good to the environment, and then they refuse to let you fix your stuff, I just cry foul."

Around the globe, governments are increasingly committed to making the right to repair the law of the land. India's Ministry of Consumer Affairs is developing a set of rules requiring manufacturers of electronics, farm equipment, and automobiles to let people fix products themselves. France requires tech manufacturers to register their products with a national "repairability index." And in the United States, the Federal Trade Commission has announced that it will crack down on repair restrictions.

Whatever the merits of these specific policy measures, they are responding to a growing sense that a consumer economy based on pushing people to discard the old and buy the new is no longer sustainable. Yet in an age in which smartphone models go out of date within months and many clothes are worn once or twice before being binned, the champions of repair face powerful obstacles. After all, obsolescence of consumer goods has been a cornerstone of the growth of developed economies for a century.

In his 2006 book *Made to Break,* the historian Giles Slade points to 1923 as the year when color and styling, so that trend-conscious buyers would keep buying the latest Chevrolet. Sloan's collaborator Harley J. Earl was candid about their aim: "Our big job is to hasten obsolescence."

The plan worked. By the end of the 1930s, GM had overtaken Ford as the world's biggest car manufacturer. In the decades that followed, manufacturers of a wide range of consumer goods, eventually including Ford as well, would

---

In an age in which smartphone models go out of date within months and many clothes are worn once or twice before being binned, the champions of repair face powerful obstacles.

---

manufacturers began to make a regular cycle of obsolescence and replacement central to their growth strategy. In the nineteenth century, companies had sought success by making products that were durable and repairable – Singer sewing machines, McCormick agricultural machinery. Manufacturing designs tended to reflect an ethic of stewardship. This was the ethic that most famously guided Henry Ford in his commitment to producing a car, the Model T, that was affordable to the masses, built for years of use, and easy to fix. At first, Americans responded enthusiastically; by 1920, 55 percent of US families owned a Tin Lizzie. Ford would later sum up his goal: to build a car that was "so strong and so well-made that no one ought ever to have to buy a second one."

The downside to Ford's commitment to durability and repairability was that it discouraged repeat customers. His competitor Alfred P. Sloan of General Motors saw the opening. Taking inspiration from the world of fashion, one hundred years ago he began experimenting with bringing out new car models each year, often varying only learn the lesson and aim for obsolescence as the key to sales growth. Over the following decades, the quickening replacement cycle for things we buy has become so embedded in daily life that it seems part of the natural order of things.

BUT OF COURSE IT'S NOT. And the vast quantities of waste that result, some of it toxic, are becoming hard to ignore. They are symptoms of what Pope Francis has called "throwaway culture." In *Laudato si',* his 2015 encyclical, Francis doesn't limit his discussion of throwaway culture to obvious examples such as electronic waste, disposable packaging, greenhouse gases, agro-industrial runoff, or the accumulation of plastics in oceans. Such problems, after all, might be solved with the right mix of policies and technologies from within the framework of consumer capitalism. Instead, the disposability of things becomes for him, by a kind of synecdoche, a symbol of the disposability of the natural world itself, "our common home," which our technological society is destroying in selfish pursuit of dominance. And it's a symbol too of the disposability of people, especially "the excluded" – the poor, people with disabilities, the elderly, immigrants and refugees, and the unborn. To resist throwaway culture, Francis suggests, requires more than just finding fixes for pollution or climate change. It demands a revolution against a modernity based on what he calls "rapidization," together with the financial and political systems that power it.

Not everyone will be convinced by the pope's analysis. To blame throwaway culture for so

manifestations ranging from the strip-mining of mountaintops and logging of irreplaceable habitats to the commodification of babies through genetic selection and surrogacy.

BUT PERHAPS GOOD HABITS can spread from one part of life to another as well as bad ones; perhaps throwaway culture can be resisted by building a repair culture. That's the hope that drives the right to repair movement. It's also the inspiration for grassroots initiatives such

---

If we treat things as discardable rather than stewarding them, our throwaway habits may easily seep over into how we treat the natural world and other human beings.

---

broad a gamut of ills, from food waste to abortion, can seem a stretch. Yet if we narrow the focus from modern society in its entirety to the lives of the individuals who make it up, the power of his argument comes into sharper view. His insight into the vice that lies at the heart of technological capitalism – its overweening desire for mastery and possession, to the harm of the created world and vulnerable others – is well rooted in Christian tradition. It's the same vice that Augustine of Hippo identified as the primal human sin: *libido dominandi*, the lust for domination. In Augustine's account, this is the sin at the root of all others, alienating us from God, the world, and our fellows. If our way of life depends on this lust, it should not surprise us if it infects many aspects of our lives. For example, if we treat things as discardable rather than stewarding them, our throwaway habits may easily seep over into how we treat the natural world and other human beings. This is exactly what we see happening, as Francis points out, in

as iFixit, which provides parts, tools, and repair guides for consumer goods, and the repair café network, which includes more than 2,500 nonprofit community meetups around the world dedicated to mending everything from tuxedos to toasters.

Many readers will be able to think of people in their lives who embody such a repair culture. For me that person is my grandfather, Arnold Mommsen, in whose basement workshop I spent countless Saturday afternoons as a schoolboy. Its walls were hung with dozens of tools and its shelves were crammed with containers of miscellaneous hardware and with replacement parts for any common appliance. Beneath the workbench stood a phalanx of the repairable cast-iron fans he'd give to people in our community, the Bruderhof, when their non-repairable plastic fans broke. For a child, it was transfixing to watch him open up a battered radio and take up his soldering iron.

Grampa, who had grown up on a Wisconsin dairy farm during the Great Depression, shared his generation's hallmark frugality. He couldn't

Joseph Zbukvic, *On the Slipway,* watercolor on paper

stand seeing anything usable or fixable thrown away, from leftover food to old books, which he restored in one of his other workshops, a bindery. (Not coincidentally, he also shared his generation's penchant for packrat collecting.) But his repair work wasn't primarily about saving money. The value of a thing wasn't measured by its replacement price but rather by the use to which it could be put, and by the labor of those who had made it or previously repaired it.

In his case at least, habits of repair weren't limited to the things he fixed. Before a bad back kept him from more strenuous work, he'd spent decades building wood furniture and play equipment for the Bruderhof's manufacturing business, Community Playthings, which he'd helped start in 1948. From the first, the company's ethos was

(and still is) in direct opposition to business strategies based on obsolescence and replacement. Grampa was proud that Community Playthings' tricycles, ridable trucks, and other toys were built to outlast by many years the childhoods of those they were bought for. And of course, each of these products was easily repairable.

This same attitude seemed to shape Grampa's approach to people as well. A lifetime of living in close-knit community inevitably brings its share of personality conflicts and hurts. Grampa had learned to deal with these in the way his Christian faith taught him for repairing a broken relationship: daily forgiveness. Throughout the time I knew him up until his death, I can't remember him ever voicing a grudge or speaking badly of anyone (with the exception of whoever was currently serving as US president).

The evidence of one person's life can hardly prove a general truth. But my grandfather's example illustrates how the throwaway culture Francis diagnoses isn't inescapable. Any repairman knows better than that.

THE CHRISTIAN STORY about the world is all about repair. It teaches that in the beginning, all of creation, including humankind as bearers of the divine image, was "very good," as God pronounces in Genesis. But through the sin of the first human

Christianity sets such confidence in the coming repair of the world that it can even paradoxically celebrate the original breakage.

beings – through their *libido dominandi,* if you like – creation was "subjected to futility," in the words of the apostle Paul. The great theme of the Old and New Testaments becomes God's repair plan for his marred handiwork. As described by the Hebrew prophets, this plan was to be accomplished through the vocation of the people of Israel, culminating in the coming of Israel's Messiah. Yet when the Messiah did appear in the person of Jesus of Nazareth, he was far more than a great liberator or warrior king. He was God's one and only Son – "very God of very God" as the Nicene Creed puts it – who had taken on human flesh and nature. Through his life, death, and resurrection, Jesus accomplished the decisive step in restoring a corrupted creation, and he gave his word to return to bring his work to full completion.

Christianity sets such confidence in the coming repair of the world that it can even paradoxically celebrate the original breakage. The ancient hymn "Exsultet," for example, gives praise for humankind's fall because it opened the path to Christ's coming:

O truly necessary sin of Adam
destroyed completely by the death of Christ!
O happy fault
that earned for us so great, so glorious a redeemer!

That notion of the "happy fault" (*felix culpa*) would long occupy Christian thinkers. It suggested that by the mysterious working of the divine will through history, evil itself can set a redemptive chain in motion that results in a greater good than existed before.

This year, as so often over the past two millennia, there are myriad reasons to doubt whether putting one's faith in cosmic redemption isn't a fool's hope – not least after the world has witnessed so many heartbreaking acts of bloodshed in the Holy Land. After such horrors, don't dreams of future consolation seem cheap and utterly inadequate?

For Christians, the answer to such understandable doubts lies in the person of Jesus himself. If he is who he said he is, then the promised mending of a broken world is assured already now. This certainty is the reason, among other things, for the joy of the feast of Christmas, when believers commemorate Jesus' first arrival into human history and anticipate his advent to come. That climactic event, according to the New Testament, will inaugurate "the time for restoring all things."

If this is true, then the last act of humanity's story, and our world's, won't involve breaking or discarding, but rather repair. And the result in both cases will be a final condition that isn't merely as good as new. Thanks to Adam's "happy fault," it will be better. ⤙

KURT ARMSTRONG

Just Your Handyman

Some people build skyscrapers. I address that damp spot on your kitchen ceiling.

F**ROM MY KITCHEN WINDOW,** I've been watching the construction of a ten-story building a block away. After a year of demolition, excavation, and pile-driving, an enormous crane blocked the entire street and extended into the sky, hoisting fifteen-foot sections of frame for the tower crane that would operate daily for more than a year, slowly lifting thousands of tons of beams, rebar, steel plates, posts, concrete forms, and glass.

My experience with this kind of construction is pretty much the same as most people's: watching from a safe distance as some high-rise tower slowly takes shape. What keeps those dozen stories from collapsing under their own weight? How can a structure of steel, concrete, and glass, all of which expand and contract differently, survive the Winnipeg weather extremes, where the difference between the summer's heat and winter's deep-freeze is 130 degrees Fahrenheit? What kinds of

Raymond Logan, *Dad's Drill*, oil, 2020.

write more, establish a greater presence in the culture, have more say in shaping the world. Build more, earn more, write more, do more, be more. Dazzled by the things others are capable of, I lose track of what I actually can do and have done.

Am I doing enough? Should I be doing more? And what should I want for my son? How pleased I would be to watch him exceed everything I am and the things I can do. Is it my job to push him to aim higher, strive for more?

I'M A HANDYMAN. People hire me to fix things. My jobs start when someone tells me about something they'd like me to build, or some problem they want me to solve: we need to put a window in the north wall; we want a tile tub surround; this sink is leaky; our old fence is rotten and needs replacing; we'd like to paint our kitchen cabinets.

Each call or email is a window into a more complicated situation. If, say, there's a damp spot on the kitchen ceiling, I'll start by snooping around the house: just upstairs from the kitchen is a bathroom. Is there a leaky valve or a loose fitting? There's no access panel to the plumbing in the bathroom, so I go back to the kitchen and cut out the wet section of the ceiling. I square the edges of the cut so it will be easier to patch, and I cut the hole a few inches beyond the wet section so I have better access to whatever it is that's creating the problem. I can see the plumbing set between the joists, and – aha! – it's not in the drain or the faucet but somewhere in the supply line. A loose nut on the braided supply hose, or a loose PEX connection?

However tricky the diagnosis, fixing the problem is always its own complicated puzzle. And then there is an inescapable intimacy to the work. I have to be mindful of the fact I'm inside someone else's home, in their living space, maybe even standing on the kitchen counter, holding a drywall saw,

systems provide sufficient water pressure to run the faucets on the tenth floor, and move enough fresh air into the building and stale air out?

There is a conference room full of people responsible for a project like this: designers, architects, engineers, contractors, builders, tradespeople, accountants, and project managers minding every detail. No one person could ever build something like this. Only a few people involved in a construction project of this scale would actually know how it all comes together, and even they count on the hundreds of workers who spend hundreds of thousands of hours putting the whole thing together.

SOME PEOPLE KNOW how to build high-rise towers. Is this what I should aspire to? My life and my work are so tiny. I feel constant pressure, almost entirely of my own making, to be more driven, to aspire to larger public work, something grander, more life-changing, more important. When I see what others are capable of, I feel like I should do more: expand my business, build homes rather than just fixing them. Or that I should

---

Kurt Armstrong is a writer and handyman and serves as community development pastor at Saint Margaret's Anglican Church, Winnipeg. He is the author of Why Love Will Always Be a Poor Investment.

Raymond Logan, *Hot Handle*, oil, 2020.

carving a hole in the ceiling. These customers have had to admit a vulnerability, and they've asked me to come and help. The problem is mechanical, structural, or technical, but my work is every bit as much relational as it is physical. The repair problem is always tangible, but it's always people I'm working for. I can fix the leak, I'm sure. But how quickly do they need it done? Can I work here in the kitchen while still allowing them to do what they need to do? Am I working quickly enough for them? Am I making more of a mess than they'd anticipated? And how perfect will they expect the drywall patch to look when I'm done?

Homeowners identify a problem, but usually I have to dig deeper to find its source. I have been doing this kind of work long enough that I have some sense of the kinds of things that go wrong in older homes, and what I lack in experience I can mostly make up for in determination and trustworthiness. I don't always really know how to do whatever task I've said "yes" to, but I accept the responsibility to assess the problem as best I can, and will write a fair and honest bill when the work is done. (Actually, I often bill to my own detriment; I still don't know how to properly charge for my work.)

FOR FOURTEEN YEARS I've been doing this. My business strategy is nothing more than word-of-mouth and repeat customers – I've never advertised. It's grown into a modest but thriving business, but it was born out of desperation and necessity, when I landed in a gap between jobs and needed to do *something* to earn some money. I knocked on our neighbors' door and asked if they needed something – anything – built in their house. "A window seat and an indoor playhouse for the boys would be nice." I've been fixing and building things ever since.

I call myself a part-time autodidact handyman, a playful term to distract folks from the fact that, on paper at least, I have no business whatsoever working on their house. I have a decent education in theology and literature, but zero official qualifications for building a deck or plumbing a kitchen sink or adding lights to an entryway. Autodidact isn't quite right, though, because for years I worked as a laborer alongside experienced, qualified, and certified tradespeople: carpenters, bricklayers, a plumber, an electrician, and a glazier, all of which constituted a kind of informal apprenticeship in the general principles of building and construction. From these pros, I picked up a good sense of how to do good work: selecting quality materials, proper fasteners, decent tools; establishing an orderly worksite; maintaining professionalism with colleagues and good and honest communication with customers; knowing when to fuss with details and when the work is good enough; knowing when to push through and finish a job and when to pack up the tools and call it a day.

I still don't mind asking for help from friends who are trained electricians, plumbers, framers, engineers, and architects. But the vast majority of what I know in my work has come from continuously saying "yes" to jobs I've never done before – I decided I could figure them out by being careful. Massive construction jobs take large teams, heavy equipment, advanced math, and huge budgets; in my kind of work you can get by with basic tools, junior-high math, honesty, a reasonable dose of common sense, courage, and, most of all, attention. In my kind of work you'd better take things apart carefully because you're going to have to put them back together again.

So most of what I know about building I've learned from careful demolition, close attention, and common sense, shot through with medium-to-high anxiety as I mess with people's homes. I've learned how to build by learning to take things apart, minding the various elements, noting materials and fasteners and what goes where, checking level and plumb (or approximations thereof in the old houses I typically work in). I'm learning how to communicate well with customers, to walk the line between the sort of exaggerated know-how that makes me look more qualified than I actually am, and the reflexively self-effacing disclaimers that come all too naturally to me and make people question whether they should have hired me at all.

I have renovated a dozen bathrooms and built kids' beds, basement walls, frames for stretching art canvases, decorative wall structures, openings for new doors in old houses, elaborate bookshelves, storm windows, front decks, porch steps, boardwalks, woodsheds, backyard fences, cedar garden planters, crokinole boards, and picture frames. I've built a clothesline for an eco-conscious politician, a treehouse and zipline for the four kids of a single mom, a coffin for my father-in-law and another for an infant.

My projects are modest – the biggest thing I do is gut and renovate bathrooms – but the moment I step over the threshold to work on anyone's house, it's all on me to do good work and not wreck things. It's simpler than a ten-story tower, but I carry the responsibility entirely.

I HAVE A TINY WORKSHOP in the basement of our house, where I keep my table saw and tools, and I'll admit it's a pain in the arse to haul the tools and materials up the stairs at the start of every day. Sometimes it's hard even to get out of bed and face another day of this. I didn't choose this because it's my dream job. Handyman work is not my passion, not by a long shot. I don't hate my work, but I don't do it because I love it. I do it because I love my wife and kids and want to provide for them.

My kids get regular doses of "No limits!" and "You can be whatever you want!" in school, and I resent it because it simply isn't true. You cannot actually be whatever you want. That's harmful, sentimental garbage. Fact is, the real world is chock full of limits.

The other trouble with the promise that you can be anything is that you can spend a lifetime trying to be anything, forgetting that you actually already *are something*.

Now, I am a small man; I live a small life where I make careful, modest choices. I am not an entrepreneur, an adventurer, or a risk-taker. I don't have the freewheeling imagination of an artist. Also, I know all too well that I come from a line of sensitive souls touched with mental health troubles that range from chronic everyday melancholy to the catastrophic. My mental health is like a bike with tires at 30 PSI instead of the suggested 80. I can pedal along most of the time and usually get where I need to go, but I spend a lot more emotional energy than necessary. I am not the kind of man who is likely to guide my children to greatness.

I don't know who my children will be – ambitious, driven, fierce, and singular; or content, satisfied, and peaceful. Maybe they will do great things. I can't say much to them about that. What I have to say is small, but I think it counts for more: "If I have prophetic powers, and understand all mysteries and all knowledge . . . but have not love, I am nothing." Ever since they were little, I have prayed for them at night: "May they grow up to be strong, wise, kind people who know you and love you."

I don't know what they will do with their lives, where they will go, what they will learn and study, what kinds of work they will do. I was thirty-five before my vocation started to crystallize and I began finding work that was a good fit for who I am. So I'm not going to tell them what to do or make plans for what they will be. I might encourage some things and discourage other things: "I'd feel better about you being a carpenter than an investment banker because I think some jobs are more taxing on the soul than others."

IN *THE MASTER AND HIS EMISSARY,* the Scottish psychiatrist Iain McGilchrist argues that for the past five centuries, we have constructed and inhabited a world of orderliness, mastery, and objects. Ours has become a left-brain-dominated world that prefers straight lines, predictability, and power. This has had catastrophic effects, he argues, because it undervalues human relationships. Our orderly mastery of materials is powerful, but it's secondary – McGilchrist believes we've spent centuries mistakenly trusting our engineered, manufactured, modern, manipulated existence as though we have the power to construct something fixed and predictable, all to the detriment of the inextricable relatedness of everything. God bless modernity and its many comforts – penicillin, anesthetics, triple-pane windows, power grid, silicon chips, Netflix. Without modernity I wouldn't have bananas, cordless tools, or emails from friends in Australia. But it's becoming clear how costly it all is: glowing screens captivate and splinter our attention; our capacity to harness the power of stored carbon has unleashed a slow-moving catastrophe; our water and food are polluted; modern weaponry has killed millions.

Home repair helps pull me back to the primacy of human relationship. I begin with attention: I show up, attend, observe, and listen. Sometimes the customer needs someone to talk to as much as he needs his floor replaced. My work takes care, and when I do it well, love. I mostly work away from home, but wherever I go, I am always a father to my children. They are never more than one or two steps removed from every decision I make.

I like the word "integrity." I grew up thinking it was primarily about moral behavior, and that I ought to strive to be a man of integrity. As a handyman, I've come to understand it more as a description of right relationship, that a thing has integrity when its parts work together and serve the whole. The integrity of a beautiful old house means that its systems and their thousands of parts work as a whole, from ridge cap to footing and everything in between. Roof trusses, studs, joists, shiplap, plumbing, eaves, windows, flooring, faucets, switches. A house will function as a house and a home when it is built well and maintained well,

in an integrity of form and function, beauty and usability. If it is poorly made, or when it starts to fall apart, integrity suffers. Give a simple leak enough time and it is capable of ruining the whole thing.

Every week at church, the deacon reads this: "You shall love the Lord your God with all your heart and with all your soul and with all your mind. This is the great and first commandment. And a second is like it: You shall love your neighbor as yourself. On these two commandments depend all the Law and the Prophets." Love God; love my neighbor. Who is my neighbor? I am grateful for the philosophers and theologians who have written complex, eloquent arguments. But it is neighbors, not philosophies, that I live and work for.

Every day when I go to work I think of my kids. I picture their faces and imagine their voices. I pray for just enough courage, audacity, stubbornness, and humility for the day's work. I pray for willingness to face whatever the problem is, and I plunge in. I close my eyes and take a deep breath, thanking God for muscles that are strong enough and hands that are willing, for the gift of work where I can be useful to others. And I head out the door to help provide for my beloved children and their simple, beautiful, everyday needs. ➤

To Mend a Farm

A restored landscape will be more than it was before,
bearing the marks of damage and repair.

ADAM NICOLSON

I F I LOOK OUT of the window at home in Sussex, across the woods and pastures of the farm where I live, one word comes back to me each morning: repair. Remake this place. Mend it. Undo the damage that was inflicted on it, along with most of the English landscape, in the late twentieth century, when a horrible litany unfolded of removal and reduction, an ignoring of the past, an imposing of the chemical and clarified present.

The only duty to a place like this must be to reinvigorate it, make it good, do what the world in general is coming to recognize – that undoing

Annie Soudain, *Seed Heads*, reduction lino print, 2015.

is as important as doing, that unchange can be as healthy as change, that the half-forgotten past can hold many answers.

I don't often repair things, but I know I should, and so when, the other day, I found an old and beautiful bowl that was broken years ago and put away in pieces in a cupboard, I decided to mend it. To make amends, somehow, by mending it. My wife had bought it from a woman who imported objects from Iran and the bowl had about it all the allure of that country: a purity of form, wide and full, almost but not quite a hemisphere, about ten inches across. When complete, it could hold five or six oranges or pomegranates. It was coated all over in the deep turquoise glaze of Isfahan, a color used for tiles in the pools of Persian gardens to suggest the brightness of the sea or of the water in a clear river, luminous and deep.

The bowl was in about eight pieces and the fragments revealed on their edges the clean white body of the clay of which it was made. And so: The table cleared and the pieces laid out. A good strong glue. My sleeves rolled up, hands washed. And slowly, perhaps over an hour, I fitted the pieces back together, finding in the slight bulges and ripples of the broken edges their counterparts on the other side, a protrusion here, a depression there, so that the mended edges met each other with an extraordinary and natural precision that no designer could have mimicked. These almost-bubbled contours of the break itself guided the process of recovery, as if the break were remaking itself and the film of the accident run in reverse.

It made me curiously happy. I was in no hurry to finish. The broken form started to become whole.

When everything was at last complete, it wasn't. There was a small chip on one side and a tiny, almost-triangular piece was missing, just at the point where the body of the bowl reached the vertical. Other glued joints came up to its

corners and met there, like the lanes coming into a marketplace in a medieval town, leaving a triangular hole. I looked in the cupboard where the pieces had been stored but could find nothing. This wonderful bowl could never hold a brimful of soup or stew again. Fruit could sit in it but nothing liquid. And so I set it on the windowsill with its flaw turned away and left it for a while, seeming perfect.

Now, though, I have started to wonder more about that bowl and its missing triangle, and how it might reflect the remaking of a landscape. The gap in the bowl changes the thing. It is both the same bowl and not the same bowl that it was before. It now embodies some of its history with us, a kind of narrative in the object which its smooth, cleanable, glimmer-perfect surfaces would have resisted before. Now, though, it has more: on top of all of those everyday and usual qualities, the chromatic pleasure of its blueness, the lovely substance of its roundness, it has its history of use, of breakage and mending, of being ours, of being dropped, forgotten, and then cherished. In its remade state it is somehow, perhaps only to me, the author of its remaking, more valuable than before.

Mending, and particularly incomplete mending of this kind, infuses material objects with a quality that is not quite ownership but more like a mingling of our identity with theirs. There is something of us in the bowl now, as if the bowl has acquired some of our lives. I feel like saying that where we previously owned the bowl, the bowl now owns at least part of us. Mending, it turns out, is a form of melding.

The great twentieth-century French philosopher Henri Bergson considered a good existence to be one that was absorbed within the perpetual becoming of life: "To exist is to change, to change is to mature, to mature is to go on creating oneself

Adam Nicolson is an author and journalist. He is the author of numerous books on landscape, literature, history, and the sea. His most recent book is How to Be: Life Lessons from the Early Greeks *(Farrar, Straus and Giroux, 2023). He and his wife live in Sussex, England.*

endlessly." That idea has echoed though all cultures and all human history. Zen Buddhists, the makers of the great Gothic cathedrals in Europe, the first Greek philosophers on the shores of the Aegean, modern physicists, and the Romantic poets have all understood the centrality of becoming. Nothing is essentially itself. Everything is always on the road from one state to another. Identity – of bowl or person or creature or building or place – is only the form through which the flow of the material world is currently passing.

Loss of memory is loss of meaning, and mending is one of the lamps of memory, lighting the way from past to future.

This flood-in-time is the river in which we float and mending, the love and habit of repair, is a conscious act within it, a swimming more than a floating in time, extending past into present and future, not to deny the passage of time but to make it explicit, to show that we are living within it, making our own existence concordant with Bergson's perpetual becoming. The mended bowl has been one thing, is now another, and will in time, as we will, move on again.

That time-breadth is the beauty of repair and nowhere is this of more vivid importance than in the landscape around us. We are in a polycrisis of nature, climate, society, belief, governance, and even language. How are we to speak in a world that is fraying to the point of incommunicability? How do we connect what we have been with what we might be?

Surely one route is in mending, which those who have tended to the landscape, above all the premodern farmed landscape, have always understood to be central to their lives. The ancient practice of agriculture, of shaping the growing world to our needs, is founded on five interrelated recognitions: things break and decay; there is something good in that perishing; once mended, things will grow again; mending is a form of belonging; and a mended place carries the mark of its own (often repeated) breaking.

Modern destructive agriculture, fueled by the chemical industries after 1945, abandoned this five-part vision of belonging, making, and re-making and substituted it for a one-term gospel of dominance. Care for places became essentially unitary and divorced from time: clear the ground by excluding all competitors, clean it up, and extract what value you can. The cyclicality of mend-and-grow was abandoned in favor of spray-and-run.

The ancient agricultural principle was no different than the basis, for example, on which birds equip themselves for life. At the core of their year is a phase of mending. Reduced to its essentials, the bird pattern is this: find a territory, get a mate, raise and feed the young to the point where their lives are their own and then *withdraw and mend*. In late summer, in England, nearly all the birds fall silent. They have undergone the stress of raising one or more broods of chicks. Their bodies are exhausted, their plumage often unrecognizably torn and frayed. And so in the quiet and dark of a thorn thicket or the depths of a forest, their bodies repair themselves. Internally, all the organs devoted to breeding, to the production of sperm and the laying of eggs, shrivel away. Even that part of their brain that is dedicated to singing the songs with which they establish their territories and attract their mates shrinks to nothing, waiting in abeyance until needed again the following year. The birds molt their old used feathers and new ones sprout in their place – not all at once; the birds are never left naked or

The author's mended bowl.

The author's farm, as seen from above.   Nicolson's reimagining of his land after repair.

flightless – but one by one new feathers appear until the birds are equipped again. The bodies of those that must fly south gather reservoirs of fat on which to make the journey.

For us culture-beings, there is another dimension to this. We can *choose* to repair our selves and our world. And why should we? Not only because our interests are biologically tied up with those of the plants and animals that we have been busily destroying for the last eighty years, but because the act of memory which repair represents is essential to our own happiness. Loss of memory is loss of meaning, and mending is one of the lamps of memory, lighting the way from past to future.

John Ruskin's idea, writing about architecture, was that

> the greatest glory of a building is not in its stones, nor in its gold. Its glory is in its age, and in that deep sense of voicefulness, of stern watching, of mysterious sympathy, nay, even of approval or condemnation, which we feel in walls that have long been washed by the passing waves of humanity. [1]

If a place has long been worked by human hand, it is replete with the complexity and muddle of

thousands of human decisions. Wisdom and idiocy have both played their part. Unless it has been clarified by modern impositions, a farmed landscape is a model of making do and getting by, of a gate that may be in the slightly wrong place but has always been good enough, a tree that has outgrown its hedge, a pasture gone reedy with springs bursting through its grasses. In its accumulations it has acquired Ruskin's "voicefulness." The long-mended thing speaks to us with what he called "mysterious sympathy," as if to say, "Yes, listen, you can be at home here too. This is a human place. Its mending is its meaning."

Such a landscape is not a view or a work of art. It is an intricate layering of past lives in which human and natural have long been interfolded. To remake it is not to abandon it or to rewild it but in some ways the opposite: to *reculture* it, to allow the ancient connections between human use and animal and plant life to re-establish themselves in a way that persisted here for at least half a millennium before the locust years of the late twentieth century descended.

I am now in the midst of a long program of repair in this place, of allowing it to grow back into its historical form. But what is repair in that landscape sense? It is the removal of those

1. From the chapter "The Lamp of Memory" in John Ruskin's *Seven Lamps of Architecture, Works* VIII (233–4).

influences that will not allow it to self-repair. Repair, oddly enough, lives in an ambiguous place that combines intervention with a lack of it, providing the frame within which an enriched natural life can re-assume its role. It is full of mends, and there are many missing, roughly triangular corners where something other than human intention holds sway. And so to encourage myself, I have made an image to guide me: the farm as it is now, a little bare, a little lifeless, and another of what it might become long after I am dead: full of thickness, every hedge allowed to balloon and roughen; little woods on steep slopes; no field bigger than three or four acres; trees growing in the middle of pastures; green lanes crossing the landscape; ponds in the wet patches. Amidst all of which, the cattle and sheep of the farm will find their home, as will the nightingales and turtle doves, and those people who will be lucky enough to call it home. ⟩

Annie Soudain, *Winter Glow*, reduction lino print, 2017.

René Magritte, *The Poet Recompensed*, oil, 1956

Andy Mayhew,
Author of the Sonnets of Shakespeare

He tried to do it right. ABAB.
Every time, though, he had to give up, foiled
By headstrong form, the rhyme scheme and the beat
He failed to marry. How a marriage failed,
He knew too well, two lives jarred askew, refusing
To line up. Love and love sonnet, both botched.
Nothing to show for all his obsessive fussing.
Better just to memorize Shakespeare's batch.

Alzheimer's turned his scars to cuts in water
But left him with those lines that rhymed and scanned,
And in his nursing home, he showed his daughter
The Sonnets forming in his sloping hand,
The clinching couplets that would make him famous,
Forgotten so completely they became his.

AMIT MAJMUDAR

Visible Repair

A mom makes mended clothes beautiful.

LEAH LIBRESCO SARGEANT

For GRACE RUSSO, a mother in Westminster, Maryland, mending clothes is both a quotidian chore of stewardship and an invitation to contemplation. Inside her home, she patches clothes with exuberant needlework, which overspills the original damage and overruns the garment. Outside, she applies her training as a master gardener to decide which acts of human creation honor the natural world and which must be ripped out by the roots.

Russo became interested in mending when she was in graduate school, where she had little space

---

Leah Libresco Sargeant's writing has appeared in the New York Times, First Things, *and* FiveThirtyEight. *She runs* Other Feminisms, *a Substack community focused on interdependence.*

in her budget for new clothes when hers got too thin or damaged. The clothes that most needed mending were the ones she had worn most – "I had a lot of plaid flannel shirts that were fraying at the cuffs or losing their seams," she says. It's the most loved daily clothes that need repair while the poorly-suited-to-you dress hangs pristine at the back of the closet.

Russo had always liked making art, and she was drawn to embroidery as a way to doodle and draw with thread. The first book she read on decorative embroidery was by a Japanese artist, which eventually led her to discover *sashiko*.

Sashiko is a Japanese hand-quilting technique that can be used purely as ornament or as a way to add a patch to a worn piece of fabric. The technique traditionally uses white thread on indigo fabric, making the mending bright and noticeable. The stiches usually appear all the way across the patch, not just at the edge to bind it into place. It turns the entire patch into a canvas for geometric or nature-inspired patterns.

Russo mends her husband's cotton button-downs with little rivulets of colorful thread. As the shirts get old enough to show wear, they also are finally old enough to be soft and wonderful against the skin. It takes mending to keep them in circulation when their material has reached its best quality.

When Russo began repairing her clothes, it changed what kinds of new clothes she wanted to buy. When she looked at something on the rack or at a thrift store, she didn't just consider how the outfit looked then, but how it would change as it aged and weakened. What kind of mending would it need and what kind of repairs could it support?

She looked for thicker cotton fabrics that could stand up to strong stitches. She avoided clothes made of stretchier synthetic fabrics – she didn't like the idea of wearing petroleum products, but more than that, they didn't take repairs gracefully. She even wound up checking online reviews of clothes to see what kind of seam was hidden inside a dress before ordering it. A straight stitch in a stretchy maternity outfit was much more likely to rip than a zigzag.

As she looked at each seam, imagining how she might one day pass it back through a machine, she had a stronger sense of the hands that had already guided it, inch by inch, into its present form. Until she took up sewing herself, Russo imagined that a lot of clothes manufacturing was automated in the ways spinning thread had been. But there are almost no sewing machines that work alone. The needle is pumped up and down by a motor, but human hands guide the cloth around its turns. There is nothing woven that we put on our bodies that hasn't passed through someone's hands, usually half a world away.

Russo wants her girls to have a deeply rooted sense of the work and intention that each act of creation requires.

Not everything can be repaired, or, in Russo's judgment, should be. There are items that are ready for the rag bin, and others that she puts aside indefinitely. She *could* fix them, but only at the expense of her other responsibilities. "I'm balancing the amount of work and the emotional weight of the garment," she explains. Some badly damaged clothes might get tucked at the bottom of the mending basket, where they are held in hope of a change of season, more independence for the girls, a stretch of time to let the rips bloom into beauty. Some will become patches themselves.

Repair is natural and necessary for her children's clothes. She tries to buy well-made clothes and then turn her daughters loose to explore and be active – which means their dresses make frequent trips to the laundry and mending baskets. Her oldest, Beatrix, is three, and Russo finds ways to let her participate in making whole what her play has torn.

Russo dips the needle in and out of the cloth, Beatrix pulls the thread through till it's taut. She sits beside her mother to work with her own needle on a lacing card. Russo's goal is that each of her

---

Our world can't be remade new from whole cloth. Instead, Russo tries to scaffold up better systems that are more resilient.

---

girls "grows up with an awareness that creating things takes work, things don't just appear."

A home is not a factory floor, but it's easy for the work of mothering and homemaking to slip behind the same veil of effortlessness that companies use to conceal the skilled labor required to create our clothes. Russo wants her girls to have a deeply rooted sense of the work and intention that each act of creation requires. The girls should have nimble fingers, quick to pick something up to mend but also eager to reach up and pull away the scrim that makes makers invisible.

When Russo takes her girls out to play, she looks with a gardener's eye, seeing not just greenery but the (often strained) relationships between flora and fauna. In 2020, Russo was pregnant and isolated by the Covid pandemic. She wanted to go out into nature and explore, and found the master gardener program run by the Maryland State Extension Service. Covid meant the classes were offered online, and she and her husband curled up on the couch together, baby eventually snuggled up between them, to learn about soil composition and restoring native plants.

The program ends with a lengthy exam – and the requirement to pledge to put your new

certification at the service of your neighbors. Master gardeners put in volunteer hours at farmers' markets, 4H fairs, and more. Russo has run games involving soil for little children. When she spotted poison hemlock in a churchyard, she noted the address and sent in a message warning of the danger.

Repairing the ecosystem, whether at the scale of a yard or a neighborhood, is slower work than darning a sock. At the house where Russo lives, there are non-native plants she and her husband ripped out immediately, and others that were so deeply rooted that she decided to live with them. A Norway maple is invasive, but "if you move into a house with a thirty-year-old maple, it doesn't make sense to chop it down and put in a three-year-old sapling." Instead, she looked up shade shrubs that *were* natives and would welcome the protection of its branches.

When a sleeve of her gardening clothes rips on a thorn, the mending won't make it look like nothing happened. And when homeowners and city planners have worked against the grain of the earth for generations, "we're at a point with our ecosystem where it's never going to look like nothing happened."

Our world can't be remade new from whole cloth. Instead, Russo tries to scaffold up better systems that are more resilient. When working with garments, "you see the weak points and try to build them up so that they're just as strong as, or stronger than, the part around it." She faces the same challenge with gardens – what here needs help to be resilient under tension?

Russo's approach to repair is bracing for someone, like me, who approaches fixing as making things exactly as they were. In a garden, I know how to weed and remove unwelcome plants, but I don't know what to *add*. What she does requires a particular artistic sensibility – not just seeing how something *was* and returning it to its standard, but imagining how it *might be*, and letting it gently drift away from factory settings.

So where would someone with little or no experience begin? Try expanding the canvas of what you're working, Russo advises. If you're repairing a pinprick hole, "your repair can be the size of a dime, or you can make a whole bouquet of flowers in a six-by-six-inch square up the side of your jeans." From her point of view, the smaller and more hidden the work, the harder it is to pull off well. "When you do a slightly larger, slightly looser kind of thing, it disguises the fact that it is a mend."

Our own wounds and mendings can take a similar form. Russo describes the work of tattoo artists who add art that complements a surgical scar or a serious, healed wound. Those artists look at "the curve of the body, as well as the line of the scar," she explains. The scar becomes the seed, and the image that the artist and the patient collaborate on "is never just tight around the scar, it blooms out and opens."

In our garments, in our gardens, and in our moral choices, we draw the seams of our life together. Daily practice with making and mending helps us recognize our frailties, our dependencies, and what work of restoration is required for us in our own particular role. ➤

Empty Pews

A young minister in a declining church looks for reasons to hope.

BENJAMIN CROSBY

IT IS A STRANGE TIME to be a young minister. I am thirty-two years old, and the church in which I am ordained, the Episcopal Church, has a mandatory retirement age of seventy-two, meaning that I have up to forty years of ministry ahead of me. I fully expect my denomination to be nearly unrecognizable at the time I reach retirement age. Our denomination is overwhelmingly old and white, and mostly made up of small churches in parts of the country that are not growing; our failures at evangelism and retaining the people born in our church mean that demographers predict that our numbers will hit zero

Benjamin Crosby is a priest in the Episcopal Church serving in the Anglican Church of Canada and a doctoral student in ecclesiastical history at McGill University.

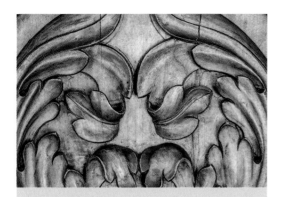

A FEW YEARS after the turn of the thirteenth century, a wealthy young man was praying in a ruined church called San Damiano in the Italian countryside. While he was praying before the crucifix, he had a mystical vision: a voice saying "Go, Francis, and repair my house, which you see is falling into ruin." Initially, the man thought that the vision was in reference to the ruined church, which he rebuilt by hand. But Francis eventually came to realize that the vision referred not just to one ruined chapel but to the church grown worldly, corrupt, and obsessed with riches. And so in 1208, after attending Mass and hearing a reading from the Gospels in which Jesus tells his disciples to go without money, goods, or extra clothing and announce the coming of the kingdom of God, Francis put the Gospel reading into practice, gathering disciples around him and founding the community that would eventually take his name: the Franciscans, dedicated to preaching and poverty for the renewal of the church.

around 2040. Of course, we won't *actually* have zero Episcopalians in 2040; I for one expect to still be around, God willing. But over the course of about a century we will go from being a large, socially and politically prominent institution to being statistically insignificant. If current trends continue, our congregations will be few and far between, and the institutions which the church has supported – seminaries, charities, missionary societies, religious orders, and so on – either will cease to exist or will have to reimagine their roles.

The collapse of mainline Protestantism, of course, is not a new story. The national Protestant churches of Europe, from which most North American mainline Protestants trace their heritage, have been in steep decline for decades. On this side of the Atlantic, their North American descendants have followed in their wake. But – and this is new – the data are not much more promising outside mainline circles. The only thing sparing North American Roman Catholicism from similar rates of decline has been immigration, especially from Latin America; the decline of Central and South American Roman Catholicism means that this can no longer be counted upon. And lately, the evangelical churches which long made the United States an outlier among industrialized Western nations for its high level of religiosity have begun to decline too. Even the charismatic nondenominational churches and Pentecostal denominations seem to be plateauing.

And beyond the numbers of adherents, we are living through the denouement of the role Christianity played in Western culture since around the fourth century: we are seeing the end of culturally supported Christianity, in which Christian churches (whether formally established or not) and the Christian religion were seen as undergirding our common life.

For some critics, Christianity's retreat from the culture is long overdue and cannot come fast enough. Conversely, some Christians see it as such an emergency that they seek political power to re-entrench the trappings of state-supported Christianity (at least the version of Christianity they prefer). Historians, sociologists, and other scholars debate the causes and meaning of this secularization, producing learned tomes like Charles Taylor's *A Secular Age* (2007). Theologians argue about whether the last fifteen hundred years of Christian history show churches fatally compromising with emperors and princes, threats rather than opportunities. Or even like being on a sinking ship and urging the captain to launch lifeboats, only to be told that the ship simply will not, cannot go under. On the basis of the functioning of the two denominations with which I am affiliated – the Episcopal Church in which I was ordained and the Anglican Church of Canada in which I currently serve – you would not know that both institutions are facing statistical

---

My experience as a young minister in the church in a time of collapse feels rather like standing on a lookout post of the *Titanic,* spotting an iceberg, and urgently signaling the bridge to change course only to be told that the *real* issue is a mentality that insists on seeing icebergs as threats rather than opportunities.

---

selling their birthright of Jesus' radical message for the pottage of worldly power, or faithfully (if incompletely) transforming both individuals and societies by the power of the gospel. Books like Jim Davis, Michael Graham, and Ryan P. Burge's *The Great Dechurching* (2023) provide careful analysis of the last few decades of church decline with an eye toward equipping pastors to win back those who have fallen away and to building durable Christian communities that can withstand the acids of secular modernity. But whether celebrated, mourned, or neutrally analyzed, the accounts all agree that organized Christianity in the West faces a crisis.

Perhaps one of the most bewildering and frustrating parts of my experience as a young minister in the church in a time of collapse has been watching the broader institutions of the church seem blissfully unconcerned with this crisis, a crisis that I feel so keenly. It feels rather like standing on a lookout post of the *Titanic,* spotting an iceberg, and urgently signaling the bridge to change course only to be told that the *real* issue is a mentality that insists on seeing icebergs as

nonexistence in less than twenty years. People may nod solemnly in response to grim reports of decline and express the desire that something be done, but these supposed desires simply are not reflected in the institutional behavior of the church. The most recent General Synod meeting of the Anglican Church of Canada, for example, failed entirely to discuss its (predictably grim) statistical report. In fact, those who seek to begin honest conversations about our crisis are often castigated for a "scarcity mentality" or a lack of trust in God. Honesty about the likely fate of our denomination seems to be seen as a bigger problem than that coming demise itself.

It's not just a matter of denying reality; I have seen my church actively make our situation worse, refusing simple measures that would aid in retaining or gaining members while praising supposed solutions that will not help, such as expecting full-time ministry on part-time salaries. This leaves pastors distracted by the need to make ends meet some other way; the Episcopal Church's own research shows that churches led by part-time ministers are unlikely to grow and

very likely to decline. In other efforts to cut costs, mainline churches have defunded campus ministries across both the United States and Canada, meaning that our churches are largely unable to connect with young people at a time in which many people either try on new religious identities or solidify existing ones. These things reinforce each other, as a church without new generations will have less and less ability to support any kind of outreach at all.

Most distressing of all, some of our church leaders themselves think this decline may well be for the best, acknowledging the depth of our crisis only to celebrate it. I've heard clergy announce that Jesus had no desire to form a religion around himself, and so it is not such a bad thing that church institutions are dying. Worshipping Jesus

is cast as a diversion from the more important work of following him, which is then understood as advocating for center-left politics. In a mainline culture that valorizes doubt as the most intellectually respectable way of engaging with the Christian faith, clergy seek to outdo each other in confessing their ambivalence about Jesus, uncertainty about God, and fear that Christianity has done more harm than good. Maybe God is doing a new thing, which doesn't involve Christians gathering together for worship – and why should we assume that it matters if people are Christians, anyway?

Here is why it matters: everyone is beloved of God, who sent his Son to bring good news to a fallen and suffering world. There can be no doubt this world is suffering from evil and despair. So why on earth would we, who have been entrusted to share the hope of Christ, withhold or obscure it where it is so clearly needed?

T O SERVE GOD'S PEOPLE as a pastor right now in the West is to be painfully clear that the work of ministry is a work of repair. This is true not just in my own mainline denomination, but across the board. Some of this is a matter of taking advantage of low-hanging fruit. For example, in a recent conversation with Father Everett Lees, rector of one of the fastest-growing Episcopal churches in the country, I was surprised to learn just how effective consistently following up with visitors and inviting them to an introductory class and a small group was in terms of gaining and retaining new members. If there are parts of the broader church that focus too much on slick production values and an energetic-but-vacuous visitor experience (and there certainly are), that is hardly an excuse to avoid careful attention to how to evangelize or teach discipleship more effectively. But more deeply, we are called to do something radical, in the sense of getting to the root of the matter: our churches need to be called to repentance and to a renewed focus on the gospel of Jesus Christ.

One of the most obvious shortcomings the church needs to repent of is its failure to take seriously its mistreatment of its own people. It has become terribly clear that no branch of the church is free of the abuse of vulnerable people by the very clergy charged with their care. Every Roman Catholic I know is painfully aware of the horrors of the abuse scandals revealed in the last twenty years: not only the fact of abuse itself but its cover-up by Catholic leaders at all levels of the church hierarchy. More recently, the Southern Baptist Convention has been in the news for that body's failure to suspend abusive pastors. Mainline Protestants sometimes like to think that our social liberalism or embrace of women in ministry prevent abuse, but they do not. Both the Episcopal Church and the Anglican Church of Canada have recently been rocked by allegations of bishops' misconduct and the failure of church institutions to respond appropriately upon being informed of abuse. It may well be, as is sometimes alleged, that churches have no higher rates of abuse than other organizations that involve work with vulnerable or marginalized populations. But "we're no worse than anyone else" is hardly a compelling message for the church to share with an increasingly skeptical world. For abuse not only damages those subjected to it, but it also turns others away from the church in moral revulsion. This means people are rejecting Christ because of what has been done in his name.

The church is also in desperate need of resetting its focus, repenting of its continued succumbing to the lures of power, relevance, and control. John Calvin was fond of saying that the human mind is a factory of idols, and the church all too often gives credence to that dictum. It is impossible not to think here of the descent of huge swathes of the Christian right, and especially Pentecostals and charismatics, into a wholehearted embrace of Trump idolatry, conspiracy theories, hostility to public health measures, and apocalypticism over the last few years. As with the prosperity gospel, the Christian faith is reduced to a sort of technique to achieve political or personal success. It is a scandal that the term "evangelical" increasingly means a set of political positions rather than a focus on the gospel of the overwhelming grace of God, not only for those who reject it but also for those who embrace it. Lightly Christianized fantasies of political domination are not only a temptation of the evangelical masses, moreover. Elite interest in fantasies of "integralism" or "Christian nationalism" shows that conservative Catholic and Protestant intellectuals are just as capable of being seduced by dreams of political power.

The mainline, too, displays a willingness to replace the content of the gospel with a political program. It happens to be a political program I

ON THE EVENING of April 9, 1906, the Black minister William J. Seymour and seven others were in prayer on Bonnie Brae Street in Los Angeles, California. Suddenly, something incredible happened: they were knocked to the ground and then stood up praising God and speaking in strange tongues. Soon, others came to see this strange and wonderful thing. As people gathered – men and women, of a variety of races – they started to be changed too. People fell to the ground, began speaking strange words that they did not understand, and were healed of their illnesses. The assembled group found a building on Azusa Street where they held a continuous revival for some three years. Neither the secular nor religious press knew what to make of an interracial Christian gathering with wild stories of miracles and the Holy Spirit's power led by a poor Black preacher. But the Azusa Street Revival launched the Pentecostal movement, and millions of Christians today have similar testimonies of the power of the Holy Spirit renewing their individual lives and those of their churches.

Pentecostalism and the growth of Christianity in China under conditions of state persecution ought to fill us with hope.

I believe that such restoration or renewal is possible even for the North American church. I am excited about evangelism, about discipleship, about church planting – and I am glad to know other ministers and laypeople, young and old, who feel the same way. There are still too many stories of lives transformed by the power of the Holy Spirit in our declining, struggling church to believe that God has abandoned us, even if our current dire straits may well be divine judgment for our sins and failures. Indeed, God promises to always be present where two or three are gathered in his name, in his Word, and in his sacraments, even in churches that feel bereft. The church may be a mess, but God's promises are forever! And fortunately, the repair of the American church is not up to us but rests wholly in God's power. We should certainly be repenting of our failures and refocusing ourselves on Jesus, taking up the tasks of evangelism or discipleship. But what is even more crucial is to pray to God that he would send his Holy Spirit upon us. It's true: our church often feels like the church in Sardis described in Revelation: "I know your works; you have a name of being alive, but you are dead." But hear the good news: we worship a God who raises the dead!

I don't know what the next forty (God willing) years of ministry hold for me. I don't know what my church body will look like when I retire, or how many of the congregations that have nourished me along the way will still exist. The scope of the crisis sometimes feels too heavy to bear. But Jesus makes it all worthwhile. Amidst the trials of ministry today, I have so many precious stories of God's grace and power, tenderness and love, both in my life and in the lives of those I have served as pastor. Our God is good and he is faithful, even when we are faithless. To paraphrase the old hymn, his grace has brought his church this far and his grace will bring it home. ⇖

Edvard Munch, *The Sun*, oil on canvas, ca. 1911

Daedalus

1.

I mastered mazes. Now I've made us wings
That will transcend my knack for complication.
There's just no medium for art
Like air—the tool and arm apart
No more, the dream of every master mason.
Work and freedom aren't separate things.

You see what I am doing, son?
A rhythmic beating, level with the heart,
Will float us far above all mazes.
Fountaining arrows will fail to graze us,
Sleeved and saved by daring art.
Now help me paste these feathers on.

2.

No maze is so well-worked with ways as flight.
Up there, son, every way is open.
To wear these wings, we must
Be dead to pride, dead to the lust
For exaltation. Don't go up there hoping
To taste the fire fruit of light.

Remember, even eagles have an upper bound.
A God may bend to kiss you, or be kissed,
But if you soar into his solar iris
You'll feel how hot his ire is.
My art will burn away like mist,
And your only way out of the maze will be down.

AMIT MAJMUDAR

The Home You Carry with You

A church that prays in the language of Jesus, scattered by war, lives on in many new places.

STEPHANIE SALDAÑA

LIVE NEXT TO a church in Bethlehem, just a ten-minute walk from where Jesus was born. Our church is built of Bethlehem stone – a pale pink that catches light in the morning and in the evening. It stands on the side of a hill, with a great, vast view onto the hills looking in the direction of Jerusalem. In the morning, when I wake up to get the children off to school, we look out the window to see the sun rising. There in the distance is the place where they say Ruth gleaned from the fields. There is the place

The church of Deir Maryam Al-Adrah in Iraq became a home, school, and laundromat for displaced families.

where the shepherds saw angels, singing. If I walk up, straight behind the house, I arrive at the street called Star, where they say the three kings followed the light to arrive at the manger.

I live next to the church because my husband is the parish priest of the St. Joseph's Syriac Catholic Church, a small community of local Christians. We are only around twenty-five families in Bethlehem, and the Mass is said in Arabic and Aramaic. On a good Sunday, fifteen people might fill the pews. On a surprising Sunday, twenty-five might make their way there. There are so many deacons and subdeacons and children dressed up in white gowns to serve that there are often more people around the altar than in the pews. The smallness has taught me that it doesn't really matter if one person or twenty-five people show up to Mass, because the bread is broken and shared all the same. There is a logic to the gospels that is not ours, one of mustard seeds and yeast, that it takes time to enter into and understand.

I was raised in the Roman Catholic Church, and the Syriac Church is new to me, something I am growing into. So is being the wife of a Catholic priest. It is both a privilege and simply the stuff of life – cups of coffee and cookies after Mass, my daughter's first communion, the smell of incense on our clothes after Sunday morning. During my husband's ordination, my daughter sat on my lap and tugged at my collar.

"Mommy, Mommy!" she whispered. "I have a tooth that's wiggling!"

"Sweetie, your father is becoming a priest right now," I whispered back.

She grabbed my collar more tightly and slightly raised her voice. "But this is more important!" she insisted.

There was something honest in her answer. Ordinations and teeth wiggling; God in all of it.

After my husband was ordained, the first thing we did was teach the children how to say the Our Father in Aramaic, so they might know that they belong in that moment of moments – when the faithful of the church still pray together in the language of Jesus during the Mass. My eight-year-old daughter can sing that loudly, and in our voices we feel ourselves participating in a chain of history. I have become used to being called *khouriye* not only by the parishioners but by everyone of all faiths in Bethlehem – *khouriye* being the Arabic title for the wife of a priest, in fact simply the feminine of *khoury*, meaning priest. I am always touched by the kindness and affection with which people say it. I was never expecting that – the way in which it touches me to be called by that name.

On Christmas Eve, when the great Mass in Manger Square is held in the Church of the Nativity, attended by hundreds and televised all over the world, we hold our small Mass at St. Joseph's Syriac Catholic Church. We light a bonfire in the courtyard, and all of us circle around it, welcoming the light of the world coming into the darkness.

On Good Friday, when throngs walk through the streets of Jerusalem on the Way of the Cross, many in our congregation do not have permits to cross the checkpoint. We hold a tiny procession in the courtyard in Bethlehem, and Jesus is removed from the cross, placed in a casket, and processed around the courtyard. He is buried beneath the altar, and we line up and place flowers on the tomb. I now feel the importance of feeling the stone against my hands.

Three days later, on Easter Sunday, Christ is risen.

WHEN VISITORS FIRST ATTEND our Mass in Bethlehem and hear the prayers in Syriac, they often assume that the community has always been

---

Stephanie Saldaña is the author, most recently, of What We Remember Will Be Saved: A Story of Refugees and the Things They Carry *(Broadleaf Books, 2023).*

About the photography: On August 7, 2014, more than thirty families from Qaraqosh, fleeing the advance of ISIS, were welcomed by the monastery of Maryam Al-Adrah, in the town of Sulaymaniyah, Iraq. At the time, the monastery had six rooms. The families were installed in the library and the church. Several neighboring houses were also rented to accommodate them. Over the months, life became organized, Kurdish and English classes were set up, and the monastery became the living space for these approximately 150 people.

All photographs by Cécile Massie.

there. Yet the members of our church are descendants of Syriac Catholics from what is present-day Turkey, from the areas around Mardin and Tur Abdin, who were forced to flee during the genocide of 1915 that they call the *Seyfo*, and that also devastated the Armenian community and other Christians of that region. Thousands of Syriac-speaking Christians escaped, forming diaspora communities in Aleppo and Beirut, Jerusalem and Bethlehem. By the 1920s in Bethlehem, after praying together in the caves beneath the Church of the Nativity, it was clear that all of these people needed their own place to pray. And so they built a church, with its pale Bethlehem stone and Arabic inscription in calligraphy over the entrance, the image of Saint Thérèse running toward Jesus carved into the altar. The Syrian Orthodox Christians, who had escaped a genocide with them, worshipped ten minutes away in their own church, near the steps of the fruit and vegetable market. Tied by history and tragedy, by liturgy and understanding, by the language of the past, the two communities remain close. Though if I'm honest, it's not only these two communities. Bethlehem

The monastery was divided with curtains to accommodate five families.

really is a little town, and everyone is close.

Over one hundred years have passed since those families arrived. Long ago, the members of our church stopped speaking Syriac as their daily language, and when they read it now, it is in prayers transliterated into Arabic letters. Many others from the church left or were forced to leave Bethlehem and Jerusalem in the wake of the wars of 1948 and 1967, until a few families remained to pray in the large stone church. Yet they still come to that church on the hill, a church that binds them to their parents and grandparents and great-grandparents, a church that deeply matters, in ways I do not pretend to try to name or understand, but that I have come to trust.

A FEW MONTHS AGO, I attended Mass on a Sunday morning in Sydney, Australia. If I don't remember the name of the church where we prayed, it is because it is of no consequence – the church was simply rented for a Sunday afternoon. There, I gathered with my friend Hana and her family, among hundreds of Syriac Catholics who had escaped Qaraqosh in Iraq in 2014 when ISIS invaded, forcing nearly the entire town to flee. As most of the town's residents scattered across the globe, thousands found their way to Jordan, and from there applied for visas to be resettled in Australia, waiting and worshipping in borrowed churches. They still spoke a dialect of Aramaic, or Syriac, as their native language, as the language of groceries and gardening and falling in love, and they had carried that language with them when they arrived in Australia. Some eight hundred families resettled in Sydney, and a similar number in Melbourne.

I have written about Qaraqosh before, about how shocking it was to see an entire world uprooted. I watched musicians and teachers, mothers and fathers and grandparents leave, part of a story in which some 80 percent of the Christians of Iraq have escaped the country since 2003. I, like others, wrote that the Christians are *disappearing* from the Middle East.

Three years into their stay, Qaraqosh Christians light candles in the monastery.

Yet that Sunday morning in Sydney, so many Christians were crowded into that Syriac Catholic Mass that people were left standing in the back. It was so much larger than the twenty-five families of our little church in Bethlehem.

The priest was from Qaraqosh. The congregants were from Qaraqosh. Young boys went up to recite the prayers of the faithful, speaking English with perfect Australian accents.

The Christians of the Middle East weren't *disappearing*. They were moving, starting over, still linked to the past. I realized the violence of a vocabulary that suggested that the moment they left, they no longer existed. The Syriac Catholic community of Qaraqosh had no physical church yet in Sydney, and so they rented a church from the Roman Catholics, and they drove from all corners of their new city to be there, coming together, as they always had, to pray – speaking Aramaic with one another and drinking coffee.

The church was the deepest home. The church was the home that you carry with you – the home that can't be taken, the body, merged together again.

That same day, as I prayed with the Syriac Catholics in a rented church in Sydney, another ceremony was taking place on the other side of the world. In Mosul, Iraq, the Mar Touma Church, vandalized by ISIS during their occupation of the city, was being inaugurated after years of restoration. I studied the photographs in the newspaper, of the stone walls, the chandeliers, the illuminated icons. I knew that it meant something to have that church still standing in Mosul, even if very few Christians remained in the city.

Still, I couldn't help but wonder what it meant – that eight hundred families were without a church in Sydney, and that a church in Mosul should be restored though almost no Christians remained to pray in it. In the end, I knew that it was wrong to measure one *against* the other, that both were true, both were intimately tied, both were the same church, and both were essential.

They need one another. I was the one separating them. No, the church in Bethlehem with its fifteen people and the church in Mosul with very few people left and the rented church in Sydney full of hundreds of people are the same church, none more or less important, or more or less alive, than the others. It is taking me time to understand.

When I was asked to write on the theme of rebuilding churches, I immediately thought of the story of Saint Francis of Assisi, who famously heard Jesus speaking to him from the cross in San Damiano, saying: "Rebuild my church." He set about making repairs to the physical structure of the church, until in time he understood that this is not what "church" means.

A church is exiled, and finds its way to Bethlehem. A church is exiled, and finds its way to Australia.

A church, in its deepest form, can never truly be exiled. It is always.

Somehow, in losing the physical structure of the church, we discover what church really is. We remember.

EVERY MORNING I AWAKEN to church bells. Sometimes, after I get the children off to school, I climb the stairs and sit in the church, just to be in the quiet, all alone, and I can feel myself centered and rooted in those who prayed there before me. That feeling, of being bound in prayer across time – that, too, is church. It is connection. It is memory. It is wholeness in the face of everything.

When I remember, I try to root myself in all of the members of the Syriac Church, scattered around the world, remembering that we are one community. I could never have imagined that I would one day belong in a church in which so many of the faithful would become refugees. I did not expect that members of my community would be kidnapped during war. I did not expect that some of the priests of my church might disappear in the violence, never to be found again. I did not expect to be placed daily in the proximity of such suffering: to be thinking of those who remain in Iraq, those who remain in Syria, those suffering through economic crisis in Lebanon, those praying with me in Bethlehem despite the occupation, those waiting for visas in Jordan, those struggling to start new lives after being resettled all over the world.

We are one body, and the challenges we live with are in many ways not special but shared by people of different faiths in the Middle East in a collective tragedy in which few have been spared, in which many have lost their lives and many millions more have become refugees. I have learned that we must find a way to acknowledge the particular suffering in our communities while never letting it set us apart from the wider communities in which we live. The church should always be the door into a larger belonging – that of humanity, in which all of us suffer and struggle together, and all of us seek to witness and alleviate one another's wounds. The church should not set us apart. The church should help us, always, to enter in. That is what my neighbors, in their goodness, have taught me.

"WRITE ABOUT HOW DIFFICULT it is for the older generation to learn English in Australia," an older Syriac Catholic man there said to me.

"Write about how we owned a house in Qaraqosh, and how we will never be able to afford a home in Australia," he added.

"Or about how I was a teacher back home, how I had a job that brought me dignity and respect," a woman added. "And now I have only a simple job."

"Write about how we did this for our children."

"About how we are now separated from our parents and siblings, spread all over the world."

I said I would write some of that.

AFTER I FINISHED WRITING this piece, horror caused me to return to it again. On September 26, I woke up to find my phone filled with messages. A fire had broken out in a wedding hall in Qaraqosh, killing more than one hundred people, wounding hundreds more. For such a small town, it was a tragedy beyond imagining. Everyone knew someone in that fire. For our Syriac Catholic church in Bethlehem, it was a devastating loss in the family.

A bride and groom, dancing, cheek against cheek. A ceiling catching fire. The groom looking up, as though dreaming. A world collapsing.

Just about everyone who attended that wedding had escaped from ISIS in 2014, lived in exile for two years, and then returned to try to start over, even in the face of great political instability and uncertainty.

For days, my phone filled up with more and more photos of the dead. Women and children. The bride's family. Funeral processions with so many people it looked like the sea.

The groom, who survived with his bride, said in an interview with *Sky News*: "That's it, we can't live here anymore. We can't live here anymore. Every time we try to have some happiness, something tragic happens to us and destroys the happiness."

I WRITE THIS FROM BETHLEHEM, where, three weeks after the fire in Qaraqosh, we are now in a war. Thousands are already dead, on both sides.

Yesterday we gathered in the stone church to pray. We said the Our Father in Aramaic. We sang a prayer to Mary carried out of the *Seyfo*. We lit candles.

I packed our bags, just in case.

THE CHURCH has already been restored and the church is still breaking, and both of these things are true. I do not know how we will live with so much grief. Only God knows that. But we will live with so much grief. We will live with so much joy. We will live – in Mosul and Baghdad and Qaraqosh and Sydney, in Beirut and Bethlehem and Montreal and Aleppo, wherever two or three are gathered, and regathered, we will live. This church which is resurrected, which keeps starting over, still speaking the same prayer that has bound us since the beginning. ⤝

Editors' Picks

Holler
A Poet Among Patriots

By Danielle Chapman (Unbound Edition Press, 190 pages)

In the preface to her memoir, *Holler*, Danielle Chapman writes, "When you set out to write to *the people*, or to rail against *those people*, they become the whetstone for your words, and they are always less exacting than the crags of your own consciousness." It is with this brutal honesty that Chapman, a daughter of Tennessee who now teaches creative writing at Yale, mines the formative years of her life. With her we ride an emotional roller coaster where we love, then hate, then love again the souls who have left deep imprints on her identity: a father lost to the sea when she was young; a mother determined to keep living for Chapman's sake but captive to the past; a military grandfather who seems emblematic of outdated values but turns out to be more progressive and empathetic than anyone would have guessed; family friends who appear to be walking stereotypes of the Old South and blind military devotion but who are as complex as anyone else with a traumatic history and contradictory impulses.

There are neither angels nor demons here; there is neither total acceptance nor outright condemnation. While many of these memories bring Chapman shame, grief, and doubt, she remains confident of their value. "I believe in my memories," she tells us, "as if they were articles of faith; that they rivet me for a reason; that, if tested rigorously enough, they will yield some meaning bigger than themselves, and maybe even the truth." She writes in the spirit of *The Things They Carried*, a novel that receives attention in the memoir.

Chapman's richly lyrical yet incisive voice never falters. "If we couldn't contain our memories, I would make containers for the flood," she asserts, reflecting on the years immediately following her father's tragic death. Later she notes, "It's in the moment between seeing the shape of something and discovering what it actually is that metaphor and prophecies are born." The essence of the memoir is contained in a line describing an emotionally fraught conversation between Chapman and another woman: "The mixed emotions of that moment captured the clash-and-chimes sound of the word 'reconciliation,' the sound of violence passing through grief into fragile understanding." This is what the memoir achieves: an angle of repose, an integration of opposites, an acceptance of paradox. Just as those who loved her contained both shadow and light, so Chapman herself is rich with contradictions. She tells a story that in a way belongs to all of us. We are simultaneously unforgivable and worthy of the deepest compassion. We are failures, and yet our efforts sometimes salvage beauty from the ruins.

Near the memoir's conclusion, Chapman describes a family of otters creating a raft of their own bodies in an effort to navigate a flood. She makes no comment on the image, but perhaps with it she offers a solution to our national angst: Reach for one another. Recognize that we are all battling the same floods, that, as Solzhenitsyn once said, the line between good and evil runs right through the heart of every person.

—Elizabeth Genovise, author, Palindrome

The Quickening
Creation and Community at the Ends of the Earth

By Elizabeth Rush
(Milkweed Editions, 384 pages)

The first time I felt my daughter move in my womb – a movement known as the quickening – I felt joy, and then worry. Her creation was happening alongside a quickening planetary disintegration: climate records smashed, wildfires raging, floods surging, ice melting, an uncertain future becoming an uncertain present.

Personal and planetary uncertainty is something that journalist Elizabeth Rush grapples with in her decision to become a mother. Climate modeling is imprecise, and there is no model for parenting, though "we must act with both our children and more than our children in mind." So, in 2019, Rush joins fifty-seven scientists and crew aboard a research vessel bound for Thwaites Glacier. The surrounding ice has loosened, and researchers can get close for the first time. "Were it to wholly disintegrate, [Thwaites] could destabilize the entire West Antarctic Ice Sheet, causing global sea levels to jump ten feet or more." It has been dubbed the "doomsday glacier." In her Pulitzer-shortlisted book *Rising: Dispatches from the New American Shore*, Rush has documented the impact of climate change on coastal communities. Now she asks what it means to create and care for a new life in a place – or a time – that is inhospitable to it.

The science, the isolation, and the thirty-foot waves of the Drake Passage all make for a thrilling setting. But Rush's account differs from the usual narratives of Antarctic travel, in which "the same half-dozen events make up most of the story that is told." There are no conquerors in this account. Instead, a chorus of diverse voices sing of destruction and creation, of community in the face of uncertainty. The book begins with a "cast of characters" and there are four "acts" and personal monologues from shipmates. This theatrical framing underlines the communal nature of discovery and of regeneration. We do not need heroes, we need each other, and Rush's book is one of the best pieces of writing about, and from, community that I've read.

On reaching Thwaites, the crew "stand together in the difficulty of it, trying to see what sits right

---

There are no conquerors in this account. Instead, a chorus of diverse voices sing of destruction and creation, of community in the face of uncertainty.

---

in front of us." Part of its face collapses, creating new icebergs, and Rush is left wondering what the ice – unknowable to her in such a short time – reveals; what its disintegration asks of us. Once home, she becomes pregnant. She writes of wanting her son to recognize the animacy of the more-than-human world. "If I wish a child into this world, then I must also wish this world upon them."

The Quickening doesn't offer neat answers, and it doesn't glorify community or motherhood, but in the shadow of Thwaites, it poetically and practically brings these things into the conversation on climate change. Reading it with my now five-month-old daughter in my arms has been, above all, a recognition of the necessity of interdependence in crisis and in creation.

—Elizabeth Wainwright, writer

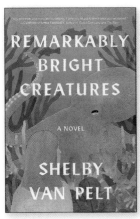

Remarkably Bright Creatures
A Novel

By Shelby Van Pelt
(Ecco, 368 pages)

Some chapters of Shelby Van Pelt's debut novel, *Remarkably Bright Creatures*, are narrated by Marcellus, a curmudgeonly old giant Pacific octopus living in an aquarium in a small town in the Pacific Northwest. The opening lines of the book reveal that Marcellus longs to live once again at the bottom of the sea, by the "untamed currents of the cold open water," instead of in captivity. Marcellus is a fascinating narrator. His wit, sarcasm, and keen observation of the humans around him are delightful and sharply accurate. Throughout the book, Marcellus is surrounded by characters who, like him, are displaced and lonely. Like the octopus in Ringo Starr's "Octopus's Garden," Marcellus "knows where we've been," and with his helpful prodding, a mystery unfolds throughout the course of the novel.

While the book opens from Marcellus's perspective, Van Pelt soon introduces the reader to the human character Tova Sullivan. Tova is a septuagenarian who cleans the Sowell Bay aquarium at night to keep busy while grieving the recent loss of her husband. The reader quickly finds out Tova is no stranger to keeping busy as a coping mechanism, something she has done for the past thirty years since her eighteen-year-old son Erik mysteriously vanished on a boat in Puget Sound. The first sentence describing this strong character reads, "Tova Sullivan prepares for battle." Here is a woman of action who also knows about war. Although the specific context here is her war against uncleanliness in the aquarium, the reader soon learns that Tova's real battle is her own struggle with the deep and lingering losses in her life.

At the beginning of the novel, Tova finds Marcellus, who has escaped from his aquarium tank and is trapped and tangled in cell phone charging cords. She rescues the octopus, gently untangling him and placing him back in his enclosure, beginning an unlikely friendship between the elderly woman and the elderly octopus. Another unlikely friendship, which involves an untangling of a different kind, develops between Tova and Cameron Cassmore. Cameron is a stereotypical millennial seeking to

---

Van Pelt's writing is as delightful and surprising as the unique twist of her octopus narrator.

---

find his place in a world that, like Tova's, has been marked by great loss. Cameron finds himself as Tova's replacement, cleaning at the aquarium after she takes a fall. Cameron can be crass and rough, but in the gentle unwinding of his grief, Van Pelt creates a captivating, nuanced character readers will feel privileged to know.

Van Pelt's writing is as delightful and surprising as the unique twist of her octopus narrator. Despite the heavy subject matter of grief and loss, there is a determined hopefulness woven into the story. It is a book about unexpected friendships, finding hope in the midst of grief, and celebrating remarkably bright creatures – both human and aquatic. Van Pelt beautifully portrays how rich and joyful life can be when, even in the face of loss or feeling lost, we find and nurture meaningful connections with one another – and perhaps with some of God's other remarkable creatures.

—Amy Parilee Rickards, book reviewer

Culture Care and Repair

The creative arts are about imagining the future as it could be.

MAKOTO FUJIMURA

In this interview, Plough's *Susannah Black Roberts asks artist Makoto Fujimura about culture care as an antidote to culture wars.*

Susannah Black Roberts: In your writing about your art and the work of culture care, you've focused on the idea of generativity. What is the relationship between generativity and repair? Can you talk about your distinction between "fixing" and "creating," both in theology and art?

Makoto Fujimura: Yes, repair can be generative, but only if we first learn to behold the fractured pieces to be beautiful in themselves. In a Western industrial mindset, what is broken, what is imperfect, must be "fixed" to be without flaws, or be discarded. In my recent book *Art and Faith,* I focus on Jesus' post-Resurrection appearances. He

not only came back as a glorified human being who has carried our sorrows and transgressions onto the cross, but he came back as a *wounded* glorified human being! That is counter to the Western notion of "fixing." The post-Resurrection, glorified wounds of Christ can open theology up, and bring art and culture-making into a new vista.

Your father worked in the field of linguistics and computing. You seem less hostile than many artists to large language models and other artificial intelligence. But your respect for the uniqueness of human creativity must put you at odds with some applications of visual AI that can supposedly create art. What are your philosophical, theological, and practical assessments of these new technologies?

Makoto Fujimura is an artist, arts advocate, writer, and speaker. He is the author of many books, most recently Art and Faith: A Theology of Making *(Yale University Press, 2021). Fujimura founded the International Arts Movement.*

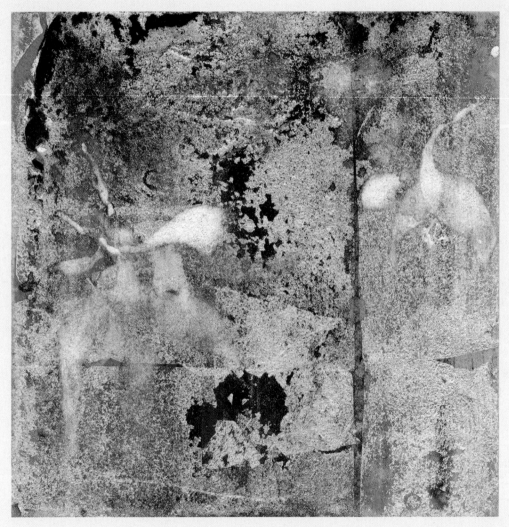

Columbines – Study, Copyright © 2010 Makoto Fujimura, mineral pigments and gold on kumohada paper

I grew up in the famed Bell Labs community in Murray Hill, New Jersey, so I perhaps have a different vantage point into technology than other artists. In the early seventies, Lillian Schwartz created computer-generated imagery, and Max Mathews created an early sound instrument machine that is now the "Max" audio simulation software still used today. What I see now is simply a huge development in pattern-matching abilities by supercomputers since these early experiments. But machines are not (yet) "intelligent," so artificial intelligence is not a true descriptor of what is happening. I see the ChatGPT phenomenon as only an extension of the pattern-matching abilities that allow machines to collect and collate billions of data, without having judgment or aesthetic skills. One can input those discernment skills, but then we are using the machines as tools, just as I can use a paintbrush as a technology, as a tool.

We have been given enormous power to either create a generative abundance of *shalom* or to destroy the world multiple times over. Of course human creativity and technology is dangerous – we can visit Hiroshima or Nagasaki to experience the extent of such destructive powers. But we have also been given the ability to discern, to correct and steward such powers. Art serves to train the imagination to seek the future, not just on this side of eternity, but, in mysterious ways, on the other. New creation does not happen fully without our making (just as the Eucharist does not happen without bread and wine). Therefore, artists and Christians are futurists; our task is to create the future that ought to be. So the question is: What are we making? What can we create today that sanctifies our imaginations, rather than uses our imaginations to seek power

and destruction? I have stood on the Ground Zero ashes in New York, pondering Hiroshima and Nagasaki. My art has been a way to explore the impossibility of this pondering.

Some people claim we live in a society that is more hostile to Christianity than in the past. As an artist and a believer, how do you respond to hostility in the culture? Is it too late for what you have called "culture care"?

In the nineties, any idea of transcendence, or even to speak of the foundations of truth and goodness, was considered tenuous, if not a threat to the established notions of relativism. In the art world, "beauty" was taboo. If you identified yourself as a Christian and created beauty, as I did, you were immediately branded as an "outsider" threat to the mainstream.

Tim Keller helped me to understand that even in shark-infested waters, we are to create beauty in the midst of a despair-filled city. The idea of "culture care" is to seek to love culture as an exile in the "Babylon" we are called to serve. Culture care is a nonviolent antidote to a culture-wars mindset where scarcity rules in fear. Culture care always seeks to plant seedlings (as Jeremiah 29 tells us to do), even in Ground Zero ashes, so that future generations will find the city, once at enmity with the gospel, now prospering because of the faithful making journey of her children. To live out culture care is to live generatively, and to create in the "fruit of the Spirit" of Galatians 5. It has always been a task for Christ's followers to do so, even in hostile, exilic lands.

Relatedly, we are often said to be in a culture war – the term coined by James Davison Hunter and now run with by many self-appointed culture warriors. You have addressed this directly, contrasting the approach of culture war with culture care. It feels as though the temptation to war is increasing: How can we understand the work of culture care in the face of this temptation? Is there a way that culture

care can respond to the increasing polarization of our time? How can culture care help promote the common life that is crucial to the political common good? Can it pull together something beautiful out of fragmentation, as a kintsugi-mended tea bowl might?

When James Hunter coined the term, he was not endorsing culture wars, but was observing, as a sociologist, that such a divisive discourse would significantly damage democratic discourse. His book *Culture Wars* was indeed prescient, and we are reaping the poisonous weeds of these wars many years later.

Yet imagine the desperation of those living in first-century Palestine, in the regions where Jesus grew up. Were they fearful? Were they threatened? Yes! There was no guarantee for tomorrow, no stability to speak of for Joseph and Mary. Yet Jesus taught us to love our enemies. To make art is fundamentally to "look at the birds of the air" and "consider the lilies" – and that is a command by our Savior from the same Matthew 6 – as opposed to being anxious about what you wear, eat or drink. . . . Art may be a way to "love our enemies," as that is the most "transgressive" act in culture.

Historically, in first-century Nazareth, or sixteenth-century Japan, or the civil war that ravaged nineteenth-century America, people had it far worse in terms of the terrible enmities of cultural division. Christians are always asked to love with courage in divided lands and tribal conflicts. Kintsugi (flowing out of the sixteenth-century Japanese feudal war period) is a fine metaphor, as we have seen it employed frequently in recent times modeled in pop culture, from *Ted Lasso* to *Star Wars*. In kintsugi, we are to "mend to make new" rather than "fix," to make the fractures more beautiful by first beholding them, and then to use Japanese lacquer and gold to accentuate the beauty of fractures, rather than hide them. As the broken body of Christ, the church must lead in the way of modeling such mending to the fractured, suffering world. We are to value people and their differences, each with a unique journey

of brokenness. We must remember that we as Christians are a mosaic of broken pieces, only coming together in Christ. Art dedicated to kintsugi generation can be the bridge to invite skeptical folks into an authentic community of brokenness, only made beautiful by our kintsugi Savior.

In the face of what many experience as both the ugliness and unrootedness of our contemporary culture, people often express a longing for beauty. How can art help address this hunger for beauty and rootedness? Can it create a people that includes Christians and non-Christians, red and blue state Americans, old and new immigrants – a cultural and political yobi-tsugi mending?

Yobi-tsugi, an extension of kintsugi that intentionally brings fragments of different sources together in a mosaic, is a powerful metaphor for our future.

First, we need a realignment of our understanding of beauty beyond a Western, industrial, cosmetic, immaculate-perfection concept toward that of a maculate, broken beauty of the East. The divide in ideology, both on the conservative and liberal side, has roots in the binary "scapegoating" of what we see as unforgivable imperfections. We see such fractures only through the immaculate lens that our ideological idols demand.

Art can bring somatic, reflective, deeper contemplation that moves us away from blaming others (or any politicians) to asking instead, "What is in me to mend, to make new?" When we do that, when we behold deeply of our own souls and the edges of our fractures, we will find that we need each other and communities (even our enemies) to find complete healing. ➤

This interview was conducted on September 10, 2023, and has been edited for length and clarity.

Heaven Meets Earth

In the birth of Christ, God comes to restore and set free every person and all creation.

ROWAN WILLIAMS

ONE OF THE PRAYERS we hear at carol services reminds us that Christ's incarnation "brings into one things earthly and things heavenly." It is an insight deeply rooted in Christian tradition. Already in the second

Christian century people were talking about the events of Christ's life, death, and resurrection as a "recapitulation," a summing-up of the entire human story. And the New Testament language in Romans 8 and Colossians 1 about how the reality

Michael Torevell, *News of Great Joy*, mixed media and digital painting, 2022.

of Christ affects the entire cosmos continued to resonate through the entire early Christian period. What happens when God becomes human is not simply an emergency plan to tidy up the forgiveness of our sins, but a matter of releasing us to be what we were made to be.

This movement into what we are meant to be involves recognizing that we exist in a complex network for the sharing of life, an immeasurable symphony of patterns of activity, each activating and enlarging every other. The basic form of the *sin* from which we need to be delivered is the myth of self-sufficiency. The diabolical urge that destroys our well-being again and again is the temptation to think of ourselves as somehow able to set our own agenda in isolation, and the greatest and most toxic paradox that results is that we become isolated from our own selves. We don't and can't know what we are as participants in the symphonic whole, and so we block off or screen out the life we need to receive, refusing to share the life we need to give. We live shrunken, hectic, short-term lives, stuck in futile conflicts and vacuous rivalries. We refine our skill at identifying other human lives, as well as the entire nonhuman environment, as competitors for space, forces that will, left to themselves, diminish rather than enrich us. We need to be healed from this habitual screening-out.

This means that the "repair" involved in Christ's coming in flesh is a repair of our relation to *ourselves*. Saint Augustine memorably said that our problem is that we are away from home; we are never properly "inhabiting" ourselves, living in our actual bodies and memories. Christ comes to introduce us to the self we have not met – the unique responsive spark that springs up out of the recognition that we emerge as gifts from the hand of God, that we are made alive only as part of the symphonic flow of all things working together, that our fullest "actualization" is to stand in and before the divine mystery saying "Abba" in the spirit of Jesus. The gift of the Spirit is something that makes us see where and how we are fed, the depth at which we are always receiving, being *given* birth. It entails seeing the persons and things around us as bearers of life – whether they look like friends or enemies at first sight.

The particular perspective offered by the story of Christ's birth is the one that so many traditional seasonal hymns underline: the unlimited

---

Christ comes to introduce us to the self we have not met – the unique responsive spark that springs up out of the recognition that we emerge as gifts from the hand of God.

---

eternal activity that is God unveils itself in the form of the most dependent kind of humanity we can think of. To be "godlike," then, is not to be in control or "on top of" everything. The most passive and vulnerable reality is transparent to God, the most forgotten and despised human presence is not abandoned by the Redeemer who is not ashamed to be fed by what God has made, by the warmth and the shelter and the milk of a human body. The moment of Christ's birth is already bound up with the mystery at the end of Jesus' earthly ministry – that God is most sovereignly active when the humanity that has been fully and uniquely united with the creative Word is nailed to the cross and can't move, when God is incarnate in a dying body, and then a dead body.

Rowan Williams was the Archbishop of Canterbury from 2002 to 2012. A theologian and poet, he is the author of many books, including Being Disciples: Essentials of the Christian Life *and* Holy Living: The Christian Tradition for Today.

The incarnation of the Word of God opens up the central reality of what we are in God's hands. It repairs that great disease of the imagination that prompts us to fantasize about being free from the body and the passage of time, free from the constraints of what we have made of ourselves, from our promises and mutual obligation, from our sheer neediness. It is this disease of

---

Once we have been healed from that lethal wound that has broken our connection with living truth, healed from the terrible fiction that freedom is separation rather than communion, the world is made new.

---

the imagination that makes us fear and despise strangers – and all the strangenesses of the world we are part of, and, not least, the stranger living within our own heart.

Without knowing ourselves in this way, we remain strangers to ourselves – and that means that we shall end up finding our own selves to be our enemy. Isn't this often what we mean by "hell"? Not a set of arbitrary punishments from outside but the bare fact of not being able to be at peace with what we are, struggling to establish ourselves on the foundation of our own resourcefulness and strength of will. The awful unreality of this is famously laid out in Milton's *Paradise Lost*: the fallen angels resolve, more or less knowingly (which is what makes it so grim a picture), to opt for untruth. That basic untruthfulness has the effect of shrinking our humanity more and more inexorably until there is almost nothing left for God to work with. We can and should pray that no being will be finally stuck in that unreality; but we are fools not to face the scale of the danger for

our unmoored and chaotic minds and hearts.

The great evening hymn of Bishop Thomas Ken prays "That with the world, myself and Thee, / I, ere I sleep, at peace may be." These words express beautifully all the levels of reconnection that we need to acknowledge. To see God in the dependent child in the cradle and at the breast, and to say, like Pilate to the crowds in Jerusalem, "Behold the Man," is to recognize that authentic humanity is not afraid of weakness. This is the beginning of our ability to recognize the dignity and the promise of what looks weak and insignificant in the world around us. As we look afresh in this way, we open the doors to peace with the world: not a passive and static balance but a peace that is the active exchange of life.

And we are at peace with God. In what must be one of the oddest ideas in religious history, we come to grasp – just a bit – the extraordinary fact that for us to be in the image of God, growing up into the fullness of love and freedom and joy for which we were created, means "growing into the cradle"; being born again, as they say, not as a moment of religious consolation but in a new beginning of grateful dependence and the acknowledgment of a hunger for the real that will be both satisfied and stimulated afresh by the constant gift of God wherever we turn. Our sin-obscured selves are repaired as we are built again into our created place and, out of that, are given the freedom to be, in our own ways and at our own level, "creators," beings through whom the one Creator transmits life and promise. The exchange of spiritual gifts that Saint Paul so wonderfully describes in the life of the Christian community is just the tip of the iceberg, a fragment of the reality in which the entire creation lives.

Uniting things earthly and things heavenly: Christ's life, death, and resurrection have the effect of clearing our inner imaginative space, freeing us from the myths in which we have imprisoned ourselves, enlarging the boundaries

of what is open to humans made in the divine image. The Spirit who is breathed by the risen Jesus over his friends makes this actual in our lives, lighting up the face of the human stranger and "the face of the earth," the place where our roots are. The gift of God, the liberating Word of God, is, as Saint Paul says paraphrasing Deuteronomy, not something far away in remote depths or heights, but the insistent invitation here and now to trust the God who is strong enough to need no earthly or human protection, free enough to become a child sucking at a breast, alive enough to embrace death.

When we pray or celebrate the sacraments of the new creation or sing Advent carols, we affirm just this promised reality: heaven and earth are not mutually remote territories but closer to one another than we could think. Once we have been healed from that lethal wound that has broken our connection with living truth, healed from the terrible fiction that freedom is separation rather than communion, the world is made new. ⤳

Tears of Gold, a new art book from *Plough,* gives voice to women who have survived violence in forgotten corners of the world.

Face
to
Face

HANNAH ROSE THOMAS

Simone Weil writes, "The capacity to give one's attention to a sufferer is a very rare and difficult thing; it is almost a miracle; it *is* a miracle," for this is what restores the sufferer's humanity. The attention Weil is speaking of is far from pity. It is a way of looking at and listening to another, a way of giving that person recognition. It requires an openness or receptivity, a willingness to encounter the reality of another's suffering.

The book *Tears of Gold* gathers my portraits of Yazidi women who escaped ISIS slavery, Rohingya women who fled violence in Myanmar, and Nigerian women who survived Boko Haram captivity, as well as Afghan, Ukrainian, Palestinian, and Uyghur women.

In Iraq and Nigeria I taught the women to paint their self-portraits. I hoped this could help create a safe place for them to share their stories, process traumatic memories, and begin to heal and reclaim their voice and dignity. As women from religious minorities, they had suffered persecution and forced displacement, and many had been subjected to sexual violence. Due to the stigma surrounding such violence, they faced shame and isolation within their communities.

During the project in Nigeria, I shared my own journey through trauma for the first time. Their tender responses, even though my pain was by no means comparable with theirs, was profoundly healing. Compassion is often born from experience, for our experiences of pain can help us understand, albeit only in part, the pain of another. The women later reflected that my vulnerability helped them to feel understood. They realized they were not to blame and need not be ashamed. The conspiracy of silence that so often prevails within communities of collective trauma was broken.

The philosopher Emmanuel Levinas speaks of encountering the face of another person as an encounter with the "Infinite." Can a portrait painting help us to behold the Infinite in the face of the other? When I truly encounter another person, in that meeting of eyes I will see the humanity of this person. What does this require of me? And what do we refuse to see? How much truth can we bear to face?

Mother Teresa invites us to seek "the face of God in everything, everyone, everywhere, all the time . . . especially in the distressing disguise of the poor." How different our world would be if we treated each individual as a reflection of the image of God and of equal value in God's eyes.

The use of gold leaf in my portraits is symbolic of this sacredness regardless of what someone has suffered. The technique is intentionally reminiscent of icon paintings. Mother Maria Skobtsova – a refugee from the USSR who died in the Ravensbrück concentration camp in 1945, having helped to shelter many Jews in Paris – spoke of the need to recognize people as "living icons."

These women are survivors, yet their lives cannot be reduced to a single violent experience. My paintings are an attempt to honor these "living icons" and to convey their extraordinary resilience, resistance, and dignity.

Hannah Rose Thomas is a British artist whose work has been exhibited at the UK Houses of Parliament, European Parliament, International Peace Institute, Lambeth Palace, Westminster Abbey, Saatchi Gallery, and Buckingham Palace. She has been named a Forbes *30 under 30 and a* Vogue *Future Visionary.* Plough *will publish her art book* Tears of Gold: Portraits of Yazidi, Rohingya, and Nigerian Women *in February 2024. See page 117.*

Leila (31)

They took my nine- and eleven-year-old sons. They took my ten-year-old daughter. They took my husband. I don't know if my family is dead or alive. I pray to God that before I die I will see and hold them again.

Leila describes the moment of separation from her children and husband as death itself. She sometimes re-experiences that moment of profound pain and helplessness in nightmares that wake her, screaming.

Leila was imprisoned for two years underground in Raqqa, Syria. There she gave birth to her daughter Ghariba. In the Kurdish language, the name means "strange," chosen to reflect that she was born into a strange world, with strange people.

ON AUGUST 3, 2014, the Islamic State in Iraq and Syria (ISIS) attacked the Yazidi community in Sinjar, Iraq. Thousands of Yazidis were killed or abducted, and tens of thousands were forced to flee. A UN human rights commission found that "within days of the attack, reports emerged of ISIS committing almost unimaginable atrocities against the Yazidi community: of men being killed or forced to convert; of women and girls, some as young as nine, sold at market and held in sexual slavery by ISIS fighters; and of boys ripped from their families and forced into ISIS training camps." (The Yazidi adhere to an ancient religion distinct from Christianity and Islam; ISIS's genocidal campaign targeted Christians and other religious minorities as well.) According to a 2022 UN Security Council report, nearly a decade later, 200,000 Yazidis continued to live displaced in camps only hours away from their homeland, 2,800 Yazidi women and children remained in captivity, and Yazidi women were still being sold online.

Lalu (45)

I look much older than my age because of the sorrow and suffering I have seen.

The Myanmar military captured Lalu's family, forcing them into a house to be burned. While the army was rounding up more people in the village, the family escaped. However, one of her nephews was killed when his clothes caught on fire, and one of her grandchildren was shot by the military as they fled.

The remaining family arrived at the Bangladesh border and crossed the river by boat. The military pursued them and the boat sank, killing another of Lalu's grandchildren. Lalu's husband was saved from drowning but became dangerously unwell – he died soon after they arrived at the refugee camp.

Lalu feels unspeakable grief for the loss of her loved ones and has been unable to move on, her mental and physical health increasingly frail.

IN AUGUST 2017 more than 650,000 Rohingya Muslims fled violence and persecution in Rakhine State in Myanmar. At the peak of the attacks, in one day alone a hundred thousand Rohingya crossed the river into Bangladesh. An estimated one million Rohingya found provisional shelter near the southeastern Bangladeshi coastal city of Cox's Bazar. This settlement, Kutupalong, remains the largest refugee camp in the world. The United Nations has described the violent military crackdown as a "textbook example of ethnic cleansing." Most of the people who escaped were severely traumatized after witnessing unspeakable atrocities: entire villages razed to the ground, families separated and killed, women and girls brutally gang-raped.

Charity

*I can recount three different times
that I was beaten by my husband
because I came back with a child.*

Charity was kidnapped by Boko Haram when she was out walking with her husband. Her husband managed to escape, but Charity failed to get away. She was held captive by Boko Haram for three years and was forced to "marry" a militant and convert to Islam. Charity was raped and subsequently gave birth to a baby girl named Rahila.

The Nigerian military rescued Charity; she was reunited with her husband in a camp for internally displaced people. Her pain was magnified when her husband beat her and rejected her baby. In the camp she faces abuse, rejection, and isolation. Access to food and water is a daily struggle.

SINCE THE BEGINNING of the Boko Haram insurgency in northeast Nigeria in 2009, millions have been forced from their homes. Boko Haram abducted thousands of women, holding them captive and subjecting them to sexual violence and forced marriage. After the kidnapping of 276 schoolgirls in Chibok in April 2014, the hashtag #bringbackourgirls went viral, retweeted by celebrities and public figures from Kim Kardashian to Michelle Obama. Since then, the security situation in northern Nigeria has been further exacerbated by escalating conflict between predominantly Muslim and nomadic Fulani herdsmen and Christian farmers. Fulani militants have used sexual violence to target women as a way to devastate communities.

Zainab (22)

The passing of days and the sun rising each morning troubles me. I am still hoping to open my eyes, as I used to, to my mother's smile and affection. I am still longing for one hug from Hana. I used to stay up late with Ahmed, who would ease away the worries and pain of life with his infectious laugh. His laughter still echoes in my ears, so much so that I sometimes turn around to see if he is really there. Wherever I look, I cannot help but remember one of them.

On May 16, 2021, Zainab al-Qolaq lost twenty-two members of her family – including her mother, Amal, her only sister, Hana, and two brothers – when an Israeli air strike hit her home in Gaza. Zainab was trapped under the rubble for twelve hours.

In the year following the airstrike, Zainab devoted herself to processing her grief through her art. Her exhibition in Gaza was entitled: *"I'm 22, I lost 22 people."* Her powerful paintings depict her pain and trauma, which cannot be communicated in words. Zainab says that she used the universal language of art to convey her voice and feelings, for others to understand the grief she carries each and every day. She writes, "They may have removed the rubble above me, but who will remove the scattered rubble from my heart?"

UNABLE TO TRAVEL to Gaza in person, I met with Zainab over Zoom in 2022. Her story stands in for the many civilian victims on both sides of the conflict between Hamas and Israel.

Tursunay (44)

Their goal is to completely destroy us – physically and psychologically. They want to take away our dignity, our humanity, and our ability to feel joy. I will bear the scars of what they did to me for the rest of my life.

Tursunay Ziyawudun spent nine months imprisoned in an internment camp in the Uyghur region of northwest China (formally known as Xinjiang Uyghur Autonomous Region). She describes multiple episodes of torture, public humiliation, and brutal sexual violence including gang rape at the hands of camp guards. She remembers how the women she was imprisoned with were traumatized by their experiences, some screaming, some sobbing, and others silently rocking back and forth after returning from the "black rooms" where the assaults were carried out.

Tursunay was able to flee to the Unites States. From there she speaks out for the women she knows are still suffering in her homeland. In her portrait she wears a beautiful traditional Atlas silk scarf.

SINCE THE COMMUNIST REVOLUTION in 1949, the Chinese government has increasingly stripped away the freedom of Uyghur Muslims, systematically suppressing their language, religion, and culture, and destroying mosques and other religious sites. Since 2018 there have been reports of an oppressive system of high-tech mass surveillance, slave labor, mass incarceration, forced organ-harvesting, and Uyghur women being sterilized or forced to terminate pregnancies.

Maria and Nadiia

The war is endless and thousands of people there are waiting to be heard in prayer. My mother and I were among them. It is a traumatic experience to have to leave home without a plan.

Maria and her mother Nadiia were living in Kyiv when the war began on February 24, 2022. Maria awoke to her mother screaming: "Masha, wake up! The war has started." Initially they were in denial, but after twelve sleepless days and nights hiding in their basement as a bomb shelter, they decided to leave the country and seek refuge in the United Kingdom.

SINCE THE ONSET of the Russian invasion, one-third of Ukrainians have been forced from their homes. This is the largest movement of refugees in Europe since World War II, with nearly eight million refugees from Ukraine spread across Europe. There has been an outpouring of support, which has led many to hope that this could set a precedent for treating all refugees more humanely. If nothing else, it has exposed the politicized, and often discriminatory, nature of refugee protection. Refugees arriving in Europe from the Middle East, Asia, and Africa are far more likely to face border violence, detention, and drawn-out asylum procedures. Who are we to determine which refugees are worthy of compassion? As Maria herself expresses it: "It does not matter what nationality you are; what matters is what you are doing in this present moment. For humanity has no geography, and kindness has no nationality." ⤙

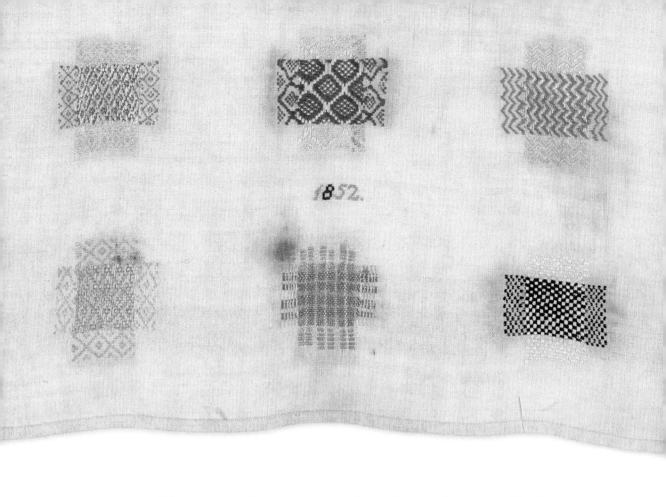

Repairing Relationships

Four writers reflect on the restorative power
of personal forgiveness.

Teresa of Ávila

Catherine de Hueck Doherty

Desmond Tutu

Jacques Philippe

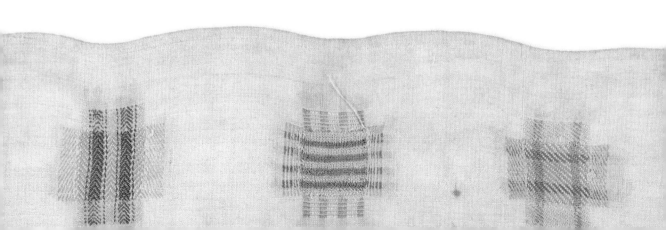

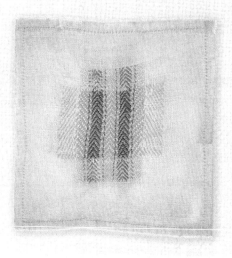

Teresa of Ávila

Teresa of Ávila (1515–82) was a Spanish Carmelite
nun and mystic.

OUR GOOD MASTER SEES THAT, if we have this heavenly food, everything is easy for us, except when we are ourselves to blame, and that we are well able to fulfill our undertaking to the Father that his will shall be done in us. So he now asks his Father to forgive us our debts, as we ourselves forgive others. Thus, continuing the prayer which he is teaching us, he says these words: "And forgive us, Lord, our debts, even as we forgive them to our debtors."

Notice, sisters, that he does not say "as we shall forgive." We are to understand that anyone who asks for so great a gift as that just mentioned, and has already yielded his own will to the will of God, must have done this already. And so he says "as we forgive our debtors." Anyone, then, who sincerely repeats this petition, *"Fiat voluntas tua,"* must, at least in intention, have done this already. You see

now why the saints rejoiced in insults and persecutions: it was because these gave them something to present to the Lord when they prayed to him. What can a poor creature like myself do, who has had so little to forgive others and has so much to be forgiven herself? This, sisters, is something which we should consider carefully; it is such a serious and important matter that God should pardon us our sins, which have merited eternal fire, that we must pardon all trifling things which have been done to us and which are not wrongs at all, or anything else.

How greatly the Lord must esteem this mutual love of ours one for another! For, having given him our wills, we have given him complete rights over us, and we cannot do that without love.

The Way of Perfection from The Complete Works of Saint Teresa of Jesus, Vol. 2 (New York and London: Sheed and Ward, 1946. Reissue edition, Image 1991) doverpublications.com.

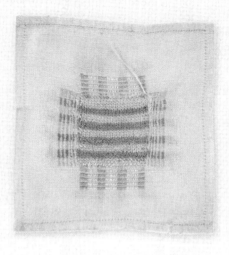

Catherine de Hueck Doherty

Catherine Doherty (1896–1985) founded Friendship House,
a house of hospitality for the homeless in Toronto, and later
Madonna House, a Catholic lay apostolate.

A MEMBER OF OUR APOSTOLATE has difficulty in getting along with another member. The difficulty is real. No one denies it. One of the classical means of sanctification is to endure the rubbing of personality against personality. That is why common life, as understood by canon law, and, in fact, family life in every home, lived properly according to God's design, is called the greatest school of sanctity. It is considered the fastest means of growing in charity and self-discipline, as well as in dying to self. This is where each one of us feels the cross. It bites deeply, and dimly we begin to understand the pain of Christ. . . .

Getting along with various people in one house is the hardest thing that any one of us can do, even though we love them very much. Nevertheless, if we have even the slightest understanding of what we do to Christ in our brethren, we would not indulge in any kind of griping. Griping is destructive, critical, and uncharitable.

One piece of advice I give to you: When you feel like griping about someone else, stop. Say a Hail Mary and think. How much material for griping does this person have about you? If you are honest with yourself, that should silence you pronto!

Catherine de Hueck Doherty, *Dearly Beloved: Letters to the Children of My Spirit* (Combermere, ON: Madonna House Publications, 1988), 55–59.

Stories, ideas, and culture to inspire faith and action

1 year (4 issues) just $36!

Includes FREE access to *Plough*'s digital version, archives, and ebooks

☐ **Payment Enclosed**   ☐ **Bill Me**

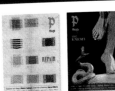

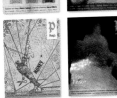

NAME

ADDRESS

CITY   STATE   ZIP

BND38

EMAIL (FOR E-NEWSLETTER AND UPDATES)

www.plough.com/subspecial

Please allow 4-6 weeks for delivery of your first issue. *Plough Quarterly* is $48 per year by single copy. For faster service call 1-800-521-8011 or go to www.plough.com/subspecial.

led the Truth and Reconciliation Commission, which investigated apartheid-era human rights violations.

*B*ELIEVERS SAY that we might describe most of human history as a quest for that harmony, friendship, and peace for which we appear to have been created. The Bible depicts it all as a God-directed campaign to recover that primordial harmony when the lion will again lie with the lamb and they will learn war no more because swords will have been beaten into plowshares and spears into pruning hooks (Isa. 2:4). Somewhere deep inside us we seem to know that we are destined for something better. Now and again we catch a glimpse of the better thing for which we are meant – for example, when we work together to counter the effects of natural disasters and the world is galvanized by a spirit of compassion and an amazing outpouring of generosity; when for a little while we are bound together by bonds of a caring humanity, a universal sense of ubuntu; when victorious powers set up a Marshall Plan to help in the reconstruction of their devastated former adversaries; when we establish a United Nations organization where the peoples of the earth can parley as they endeavor to avoid war; when we sign charters on the rights of children and of women; when we seek to ban the use of antipersonnel land mines; when we agree as one to outlaw torture and racism. Then we experience fleetingly that we are made for togetherness, for friendship, for community, for family, that we are created to live in a delicate network of interdependence.

There is a movement, not easily discernible, at the heart of things to reverse the awful centrifugal force of alienation, brokenness, division, hostility, and disharmony. God has set in motion a centripetal process, a moving toward the center, toward unity, harmony, goodness, peace, and justice, a process that removes barriers.

Desmond Tutu, *No Future without Forgiveness* (New York: Doubleday, 1999), 264–265.

Jacques Philippe

Fr. Jacques Philippe (b. 1947) is the author of many books on spirituality, including *Trusting God in the Present* (2022).

THERE ARE TIMES in every life when we find ourselves in situations of trial and difficulty, either affecting us or someone we love. We can do nothing. However much we turn things over and examine them from every angle, there is no solution. The feeling of being helpless and powerless is a painful trial, especially when it concerns someone close to us: to see someone we love in difficulties without being able to help is one of the bitterest sufferings there is.

Many parents experience it. When children are small, there is always a way of intervening, helping them. When children are older and no longer heed advice, it can be terrible for parents to see their sons or daughters turning to drugs or launching destructive love affairs. Much as the parents want to help, they cannot. At such times we should tell ourselves that even if we apparently have no way of intervening, we still, despite everything, can continue to believe, hope, and love. We can believe that God will not abandon our child and our prayer will bear fruit in due course. We can hope in the Lord's faithfulness and power for everything. We can love by continuing to carry that person in our heart and prayer, forgiving him and forgiving the wrong done to him and expressing love in every way available to us, including trust, self-abandonment, and forgiveness. The more devoid of means our love is, the purer and greater it is. Even when externally there is nothing to be done, we still have inner freedom to continue to love. No circumstance, however tragic, can rob us of that. For us, this should be a liberating and consoling certainty amidst the trial of powerlessness. ➤

Jacques Philippe OP, *Interior Freedom*, trans. Helena Scott (New York: Scepter Publishers, 2007), 58–59.

CARLO GÉBLER

If Prisons Could Rehabilitate

Perhaps some things can't be repaired, but that
doesn't mean we shouldn't try.

REPAIR, REPAIR. OH, BLESSED WORD. Something is a bit wonky, or even broken entirely. Then, it is repaired. And then it is, as the saying goes, "as good as new." How could the broken revert to what it had been before? This has always baffled me, but not nearly as much as the claim that sometimes the broken thing, once repaired, was actually even better. A broken bone, for instance. I remember teachers explaining to me in primary school: the bone, once it knitted back together, would be stronger than ever, said the teachers. Ah, the power of the body, they told me.

Carlo Gébler is a novelist, biographer, and playwright. His novels include The Innocent of Falkland Road *and* The Dead Eight. *In 2019 he published a retelling of* Aesop's Fables, *and in 2021,* I, Antigone, *an intriguing new take on the Oedipus myth. He lives in Northern Ireland with his wife and children.*

They talked a lot of other guff as well, these dispensers of lore. I swallowed their guff, of course. They were adults and I was a minor. I had no idea there was nothing innocent about their rhetoric, although it did have a perverse generosity about it. They meant well, my elders, my superiors. The thing is, they knew what was coming – it was death. Furthermore, they knew that death, the

---

Unless a prison system commits itself to rehabilitation, not just punishment, it can't do what it's supposed to do according to the writing on the outside of the tin.

---

great unspoken and unacknowledgeable horror, was the dreadful culmination of bodily mishaps that were unrepairable. So, of course, the adults of my childhood were keen to emphasize the efficacy of repair. Anything but death for them; their encomiums of repair were as much to cheer themselves up as to inoculate me.

What the teachers started in primary school was augmented as I entered adolescence. The newspapers I read, the programs I watched, the radio shows I listened to, and the teachers who continued my education all told me the same story in different ways. It went like this: In the country I lived in, Britain, repair was ongoing, producing slow but steady progress. And it was ever thus; it had been going like this forever. Despite the odd reverse (always rectified in the end) the overall direction of travel had always been one way: upward. By the time I started work in 1979 (I was twenty-five), these beliefs were deeply embedded: life might not be easy but nothing stayed broken; everything eventually mended. I suppose this can be characterized as optimism, and that in my early adulthood I would have been characterized as an optimist.

MY EXPERIENCES at home growing up should have taught me otherwise. During my childhood and early adolescence there was precious little conversational traffic between me and my dad. But I was an ardent eavesdropper, and I did pick up a few things about his autobiography. I learned that his own father, Adolf, had been imprisoned as an enemy alien from 1914 to 1919 – a Czech with Austro-Hungarian papers, he was from the wrong side in World War I. Shortly after Adolf's arrest in Dublin, my father was born, and for the next five years he had his mother all to himself. Neither of the camps in which my grandfather was detained – in Oldcastle, County Meath, and later on the Isle of Man – permitted family visits. So, when Adolf finally returned to Dublin in 1919, his five-year-old son, my father, was appalled. He never attached to his father. That is why, I think, my father and I never really had that bond either. Dysfunction, as we know (or at least believe), cascades through the generations. Many things damaged my father, but the thing that did him the most harm was his father being in prison.

So, in the nineties, when I was invited to work in Northern Ireland's prison system as a teacher of creative writing, I knew I had to do it. By working with prisoners, I could help fathers to repair – there's the word again – their ruptured or broken or attenuated relationships with their sons. I did think about the daughters too, and the wives and mothers, but right down in the kernel of my being the impulse sprang directly from my own family history. As a prison teacher I would be repairing the damage prison did to the father-son relationship. I realize now this included some magical thinking: I felt if I could repair the lives of others, it would somehow fix what was broken in my own.

I started teaching prisoners in 1995 (I was forty-one) and I haven't stopped; currently, I work for the Prison Arts Foundation, a Belfast-based charity. Many prisons offer creative writing classes because it is thought that this kind of self-expression can generate repair, or, to use the penal jargon, "catalyze rehabilitation." There is certainly a need for repair. As I learned from listening to prisoners – and prisoners, contrary to common belief, are truth-tellers more often than dissemblers – they had caused all kinds of chaos. Besides the catastrophic ruptures in their own families' lives, there was the harm caused by their offenses: lives lost, victims traumatized, businesses destroyed. And though they had been punished, rarely had the mess they'd left behind outside been properly repaired. Yes, there had been a court process and, in some cases, compensation might have been paid to the victim, but ninety-nine times out of a hundred these repairs were never sufficient, never enough. So much of the consequences of an offender's offending went unrepaired. And the prisoners themselves, who had invariably led lives that also called out to be repaired, were rarely if ever repaired either.

And, of course, if you fail to repair, you shouldn't be surprised if catastrophe ensues. Prison is, according to popular belief (among those who believe in prisons), supposed to rehabilitate inmates. Recidivism rates, however, tell a different story. If prison is so brilliant, why would so many released prisoners re-offend? Many people cleave to the fantasy that if prison were even more punitive, that would dissuade released prisoners from re-offending. But after twenty-eight years of teaching, I have yet to hear a single prisoner tell me he was improved by punishment. Nobody has ever said to me, "Suffering made me better." If anything, it has been the opposite, "Suffering made me worse. It made me want to kick against the system." On the other hand, what prisoners have said when we have gotten to the subject of the benefits of prison (and I have had such conversations) is that kindness, tolerance, and humane interaction were the beginning of their transformation, and when it came to deep repair, it was education that did it most.

Well, the beady reader might at this moment be thinking: How does this writer who so believes in repair through education explain his failure (and the failure of all teachers) to curb recidivism? After all, he doesn't seem to have done much good with this creative writing malarkey, has he? It's true, I haven't, but not for want of will. And here's why: unless a prison system commits itself wholeheartedly to rehabilitation, rather than mostly focusing on dealing out punishment with just a little bit of education on the side, it can't do what it's supposed to do according to the writing on the outside of the tin. It can't repair the broken (and all prisoners are broken; yes, they've broken others but they are also themselves all broken) and if you don't have a complete repair culture, then the broken will just remain broken and they will go on breaking others.

EVERY LIFE has a major event or two; something unexpected and unplanned occurs; not necessarily a Damascene conversion but a moment that, looking back, you realize was a great gift from the universe.

For me, entering prisons was that major event, the greatest gift in my life after my marriage and my children. It taught me a huge amount, and one of the most important lessons I learned is that prisoners don't react well to civilians – in this case teachers of creative writing – who openly declare they have designs on their students' psyche. Telling prisoners, "I'm here to help rehabilitate you" is the quickest way to empty a classroom. Far better are statements such as, "This is what I have to offer. You can take it or leave it – it's entirely up to you." By having no overt expectations put on them and no pressure to achieve results, the prisoners I taught were left free to focus on the writing. And when they were left free, sometimes something happened; some aspect of the prisoner's internal life was changed for the better as a consequence of reading or writing. And, yes, sometimes nothing happened. There was no repair. Nothing changed. But the repair that did come about through those classes – the kind that happens organically and is unforced – is, I discovered, the best kind.

Nearly half a century on, the twenty-five-year-old optimist I once was has turned pessimist. The views and certainties I once held – that nothing stays broken, that everything eventually is mended – aren't shared by the sixty-nine-year-old writing this. I'm appalled and troubled by what I see around me. Everywhere I look, I see the need for repair. The scale of what is broken is so great, I feel overwhelmed when I try to think through what I can do about it. And once I feel overwhelmed it isn't long before I feel panic-stricken and paralyzed. Considering our vast problems always leads me to a place where I know if I keep on struggling and fretting and striving and planning, I'll end up unable to function. So, I remind myself that if I want to change things, I need to remember what I've learned in prison. I have to give up any idea of being effective and getting results. That improvement program must go and, in its place, I need to simply concentrate on writing and teaching in the hope (but not the expectation) that repair may follow. May. May. I can't guarantee it will and I can't force it. But I have hope that it may, that it might.

In this hope I am not alone. I often think of the final passages of George Eliot's *Middlemarch*: Dorothea's hard-won understanding "that the growing good of the world is partly dependent on unhistoric acts" and that at least half of the good that accrues comes from those "who lived faithfully a hidden life." One has to admire a writer (George Eliot) who doesn't make immodest and preposterous claims; she admits the hidden people's work only does about half the job. Eliot knows activists are part of the picture, but she's writing here for those at the other end of the spectrum, among whom I number myself and my students. I'd like to think my prison classes are "unhistoric" in Eliot's sense: unshowy and undemonstrative, private work properly done, with no overt agenda. I write to the best of my ability; I teach to the best of my ability. And somewhere out in the universe – unplanned, unscheduled – repair occurs, but not because of my actions. It just happens. ⤳

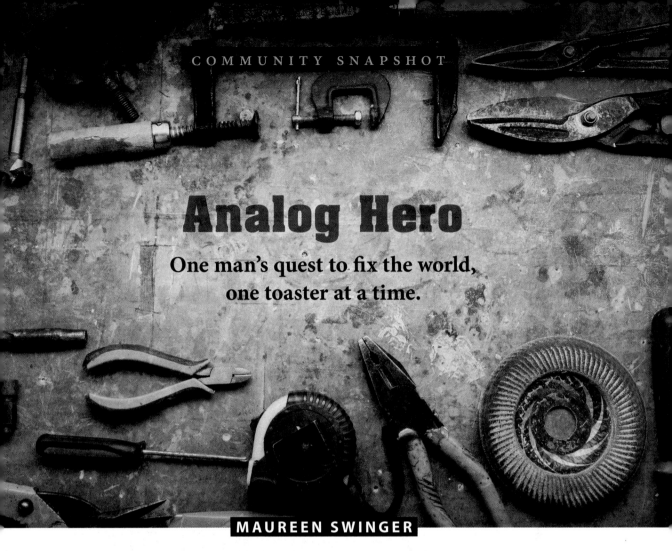

Analog Hero

One man's quest to fix the world, one toaster at a time.

MAUREEN SWINGER

MISSING: CORDLESS DRILL #2 HAS BEEN OUT FOR THREE WEEKS. BRING IT BACK.

If you had toured through the coffee-break room of the Fox Hill Bruderhof's communal wood shop anytime in the last ten years, you would likely have seen these words or similar scrawled in capital letters on the whiteboard stationed near the coffee urn. It's a useful announcement board for birthdays and other local news, but my dad, Jeremy Bazeley, frequently employed it to recall lost power tools to their rightful shelf in the maintenance building.

People would chuckle at the urgent missive – except for the guy who had left the drill sitting at home for the last three weeks, always a bit too busy to return it. He would have a moment of conscience, and the tool would be in its appointed cubby by the next morning.

My dad's notes are not intended to be shouty; he always writes in capitals – direct, concise, no frills. That's who he is: a man of many thoughts but

Maureen Swinger is a senior editor at Plough. *She lives at the Fox Hill Bruderhof in Walden, New York, with her husband, Jason, and their three children.*

> Watching him work is like seeing a maestro reaching for the woodwinds and then the strings, with each section poised and ready for their entry.

generally few words. At his own home and hearth, he likes to sit and listen to the general hubbub of three generations sharing dinner chat. But he might casually lob a dangerously dry pun into a conversational pause, without a twinkle or a smirk or any other wind-up. Whether general side-splitting ensues, or dull groans, he goes on eating. It's been that way for as long as I can remember.

We also have family one-liners dating back forever. On encountering each other somewhere around the community, one of us has to ask, "How's by you the gold rush?" To which the other, if all is truly well, must respond, "More rush than gold." Apparently it comes from an old Yiddish folktale. But it stands in for a lot of other words, and the day he doesn't ask me that is a day I don't want to think about.

This is a man who usually lets his actions do the talking. We kids remember frequent family hours interrupted by a panicked call, and he'd disappear in a matter of seconds to deal with any emergency from a generator that wouldn't start in a thunderstorm to a communal-size washing machine that had gone on strike, when it darn well knew it was supposed to wash twelve families' laundry that day. (There are many good reasons for sharing large machinery, but the downside is that dysfunction affects everyone.)

We rarely had a toy he couldn't fix or a Walkman (a what?) that didn't get a new lease on life. We took it for granted that Dad could fix it, and of course we boasted about his skills to friends who then brought their equipment for a makeover. His workshop became a hospital

Jeremy Bazeley in his workshop.

for toasters, vacuum cleaners, sound systems, blenders – you name it, he had a wrench to fit. He would have been justified in saying he didn't have time, but I never heard him say it.

This has always been his way of making the world a better place, and I have a hunch that he takes a bit of a perverse delight in outwitting big business and built-in obsolescence. I've seen him absent-mindedly pat a stereo on the head as it went out the door: "Live on! Play another song!"

This is fitting, because wherever his workshop has landed up over the years – basement, garage, or most recently a man cave directly off the living room – you can hear Merle Haggard or Johnny Cash booming through the floors or walls. The mixtape we made him for his birthday back when mixtapes were a thing was titled "From under the Workbench." (Also under the workbench is a cache of every type of battery that can fit in a multi-compartment tool bin.)

If I were making that playlist today, I'd have to include Mark Erelli's "Analog Hero":

He's the fix-it man, yeah, the fix-it man,
He can't put it back together, then it was never
  worth a damn.
Maybe he's crazy for trying to save what's
  already gone,
Or just an analog hero in a world full of zeroes
  and ones.

Looking at him bent over his work these days, you'd have no idea that he is mostly blind. He also can hardly hear, and we tease him that it's Merle Haggard's fault. He directs bright lights and the occasional magnifying glass at his work, and the fingers and tools still know exactly what to do. It helps that every last tool is in its rightful place within arm's reach, next to a printed label so it knows where to return. Watching him work is like seeing a maestro reaching for the woodwinds and then the strings, with each section poised and ready for their entry.

During Covid lockdown, he set up his shade arbor and picnic area for appliance drop-offs and repair. He didn't sit around wishing he could go to the maintenance shop; the shop came to him. Once a six-foot-tall warming oven got rattled down the gravel path to his house from the communal kitchen, and rattled back again in the evening. Next it was the panel for an electric fence at the farm.

One of the financial stewards here at Fox Hill started tallying up the savings one elderly, visually impaired, and determined fix-it man could rack up by just doing his thing, and it didn't take long to run into five digits.

Dad is about to turn seventy-nine, and he and Mom recently moved to a Bruderhof in Pennsylvania where my younger brother lives with his wife and four kids. Walking is harder for my dad now, so I'm glad he's within a son's reach (when he's not whizzing off on his golf cart to go fix something).

Recently a friend was rummaging through the maintenance building and found a standing work lamp with a label on its base, printed in Dad's signature capitals: THIS LITTLE LIGHT IS MINE. When he brought it over, I couldn't stop the laughter from erupting, but I was suddenly blinking back tears as well. It's not his lamp anymore, and of course it never was, since Bruderhof folks share household goods in common. But it gave me joy to see his label, riffing on a song lyric to make a point. All things have a place and a usefulness; they ought to be findable in that place so they can be put to good use. And so, I suppose, should we. ⇝

Jonah Calinawan, *Dark Night*, cyanotype on paper, 2020

Ifs Eternally

Maybe we don't have to figure it all out.

CHRISTIAN WIMAN

WHO COULD GUESS that one of life's most piercing discoveries would be a kind of edgeless entropy, this feeling – or is it a *lack* of feeling? – slowly creeping into all the crannies of your consciousness, a kind of claustrophobic panic that neither the events of your life, nor the people therein, nor the whole "million-petaled flower of being here" have added up to anything at all? What is the final revelation that life grants you? That there will be no final revelation.

There is no steady unretracing progress in this life; we do not advance through fixed gradations, and at the last one pause: – through infancy's unconscious spell, boyhood's thoughtless faith, adolescence's doubt (the common doom), then scepticism, then disbelief, resting at last in manhood's pondering repose of If. But once gone through, we trace the round again; and are infants, boys, and men, and Ifs eternally.

—Herman Melville, *Moby-Dick*

Fair enough. A clear-eyed acknowledgment of this seems to me both bracing and necessary. And insufficient. The revelation we want – or at any rate the revelation we need – is not ultimate, but intimate. There is no culmination that a life is heading toward, no blaze of radiance of which all our itchy intuitions and perishable epiphanies have been but sparks. Revelations there are, though. Those intuitions and epiphanies are real, and our reactions to them can be, in the moment, so total and unselfconscious that they warrant the name of – if they need a name at all – faith. But they fade, those moments, and we relapse into the vertiginous Ifs we are. What one wants as one grows older is some assurance that between the endless errands that crush the soul and the sudden warbler that ignites it, between the bills and births and meals and funerals, all the graces and losses of any life attended to no matter how erratically or imper-fectly – under it all there *must* exist some intact tissue of meaning. Not meaning such as one might

---

Christian Wiman is the author of numerous books of poetry, prose, and poetry in translation. His latest book is Zero at the Bone: Fifty Entries against Despair *(Farrar, Straus and Giroux, 2023). Wiman teaches at Yale Divinity School and the Institute of Sacred Music, and resides in New Haven, Connecticut with his wife and twin daughters.*

fully articulate or grasp, but a deep instinctive sense, an *assurance*, that in the "incorrigibly plural" swirl of life there abides some singularity of being, however fleeting its presence:

SNOW

The room was suddenly rich and the great
  bay-window was
Spawning snow and pink roses against it
Soundlessly collateral and incompatible:
World is suddener than we fancy it.

World is crazier and more of it than we think,
Incorrigibly plural. I peel and portion
A tangerine and spit the pips and feel
The drunkenness of things being various.

And the fire flames with a bubbling sound for world
Is more spiteful and gay than one supposes—
On the tongue on the eyes on the ears in the palms of
  one's hands—
There is more than glass between the snow
  and the huge roses.

—Louis MacNeice

This poem is balanced between reception and perception, between the sensory epiphanies out of which any sense of existential unity emerges and the formulations of reality made by the mind. These latter perceptions are not detached from reality – the poet is, like any responsible philosopher or theologian, in it up to his eyeballs – but they are secondary. I take the "more than" of the last line to be a reference to consciousness, which both connects us to, and separates us from, reality. To say that there is more than glass between the snow (chaos) and the huge roses (artificially created and sustained, an image of human beauty) is both to celebrate and lament an instant when this seemed not to be the case.

It's the form of art that enables perception here. The perception is of chaos, at least from any singular human perspective, an existence so various that the human mind will never master it

(there is *more* than glass or consciousness between the snow and the huge roses). And yet that incorrigible plural has been, if not mastered, at least entered; if not understood, at least undergone. And one's vision has changed: the poem becomes a lens through which we see all that we are unable to see. An acknowledgment of this revelation and this limitation is the basis of – the ground for – faith. I wouldn't necessarily say that a denial of this vision and its implications is a denial of God. (The word "God," too, can be both accomplishment and failure, but is only sometimes, the rarest times, what it really ought to be, a beautiful fusion of both.) What I would say, though, is that a denial of this transcendent vision is a denial of reality itself. And since any individual life is part of that reality, as chaotically atomic as snow and roses, why should it be a surprise that we are Ifs eternally? A single tangerine ("I spit the pips") is enough to inspire – and then to defeat – a philosophy of life.

∞

Let me not have a life to look at, the way we look
at a life we build to look at, in the world belief
gives us to understand, a snowman life.

—William Bronk, "On *Credo Ut Intelligam*"

∞

THE THING ABOUT CHRISTIANS, says the philosopher Alain, is that looking them in the eyes one senses that *they* don't believe it. This is, in my experience and apart from the obviously insane, often accurate. But so is the reverse: look deep in the eyes of the avid atheist and you sense a quiver in the iron cage of conviction, a tiny – but ineradicable – *If*.

∞

TERRENCE MALICK'S FILM *The Tree of Life* attempts to give a picture of wholeness that counters the modern sense of absolute atomization

and – because of that sense – anomie. Thus the movement in that film from scenes of ordinary domestic life to cosmic creation, from a howling baby to a hungry dinosaur, from the startling, stabbing particularity of childhood to the soft gauze of a not-quite-credible heaven. This effort toward cumulative vision is conspicuous in the film, perhaps too much so at times, but what is most memorable about *Tree of Life* in the end is not its unified vision, but the intuition it enables (and it must remain an intuition) that all of life and creation might inhere, and cohere, within an instant – and that the instant is, so to speak, imperishable; it remains not simply accessible to memory but viscerally available. Memory, trauma experts tell us, is a matter of nerves. Trauma can,

some studies suggest, leave its mark on our DNA, and its effects can survive not only our accidental unconsciousness and willful oblivion, but even our physical deaths. The sins of the fathers, it turns out, are quite literally visited upon the children, whose cells retain traces of traumas that never happened to them. (The studies that address this transmission all seem to focus on negative experience, but must we assume that our moments of extreme joy do not echo in the gleeful shrieks of our children's children?) It's not the wholeness of scale or scope one feels in the wake of Malick's movie, but the wholeness of these minute and immense, these joyful and terrifying, these discrete and seamless scraps of reality. In the long middle sections of the film set in central Texas,

it's as if time were tangible, as if childhood were a substance you could touch and taste and – herein lies the film's greatness – never lose.

∞

NEVER LOSE? Most people believe that one of the reliefs (facile distortions, the atheist would say) that religion promises is just the kind of panoptic vision I've been talking about. Religion is the very thing that puts all of our experiences in context; it makes life *mean*. But in fact this is just what faith ought to free a person from: the *need* for this kind of seeing, the compulsion to believe that truth is reductive. This is in fact the stale hell of modern scientific materialism, which is by no means confined to science.

In all the thoughts, feelings, and ideas which I form about anything, there is wanting the something universal which could bind all these together in one whole. Each feeling and each thought lives detached in me, and in all my opinions about science, the theater, literature, and my pupils, and in all the little pictures which my imagination paints, not even the most cunning analyst will discover what is called the general idea, or the god of the living man. And if this is not there, then nothing is there. In poverty such as this, a serious infirmity, fear of death, influence of circumstances and people would have been enough to overthrow and shatter all that I formerly considered as my conception of the world, and all wherein I saw the meaning and joy of my life.

—Anton Chekhov, "A Boring Story," trans. Richard Pevear and Larissa Volokhonsky

Jonah Calinawan, *Three Suns*, toned cyanotype print, 2011.

What Chekhov is saying (through his character Nikolai Stepanovich, though the identification seems pretty seamless) is that, for the person who believes we are completely reducible to physiological firings in the brain, and that we are essentially pinnacle insects, impressive, yes, prone to deviations both endearing and alarming, most definitely, but in the end as rote and reactionary as the immense machine through which we move and live and have our algebraic being – for such a person, any setback to the steady pleasure of a prosperous and emotionally gratifying existence, much less any real tragedy such as the prospect of our own deaths or the death of someone we "love" (for a scientific materialist, the word must always be in quotes) blows open the doors of deliberate ignorance behind which we were hiding: the real meaning of our lives comes flooding in, which, for the materialist, is that there is no real meaning to our lives whatsoever.

The contemporary reaction to this state of affairs is mostly either willful obliviousness, frenetic activity, or despair. (And of course these may be inseparable from each other.) Chekhov's reaction, according to Lev Shestov, was the only possible honorable reaction available to an artist who has committed himself to "creation out of the void":

But how shall a man struggle with materialism? And can it be overcome? Perhaps Chekhov's method may seem strange to my reader, nevertheless it is clear that he came to the conclusion that there was only one way to struggle, to which the prophets of old turned themselves: to beat one's head against the wall.

—*Penultimate Words and Other Essays*

This frustrated energy is what I feel in every single Chekhov story or play (Alice Munro is a modern inheritor), the implacability of a force that is both stronger and weaker than fate: stronger, because it doesn't offer any kind of coherent act or agency either to align oneself with or to resist; weaker, because for anyone who actually lives out the consequences of one's belief, it elicits not awe but entropy, not rage but resignation.

∞

SHESTOV'S COMPARISON with the prophets is misguided, I think, though it's accidentally illuminating. The wall Chekhov beat his head against was existential – essentially the Void. The wall the prophets beat their heads against was humanity. God was a given, his existence so woven into their own that they could speak with his voice. "It is not a world devoid of meaning that evokes the prophet's consternation," writes Abraham Joshua Heschel, "but a world deaf to meaning." What Chekhov sought, in the passage above and elsewhere, was respite, some solid ground on which to stand and survey the whole of life. It is, essentially, a desire to step outside of time, which, as Heschel says, is "devoid of poise."[1] For the prophetic imagination, though, there is no "outside," and the meaning of time will never be realized by denying or evading its nature. To understand this dynamic, and one's place in it, is not to "understand" God, but it can enable (Heschel again) "moments in which the mind peels off, as it were, its not-knowing. Thought is like touch, comprehending by being comprehended." It doesn't matter that you believe in such connections; what matters is that you apprehend them. And live up to them. Such moments, and the subsequent allegiance to them that sometimes goes by the name of faith, can free one from the circular despair articulated by Melville and Chekhov.

Why am I making so much of this one comparison? Because I feel that I – and many others – might be indicted by it. My instinct is to hold up something like that Louis MacNeice poem above as one of these moments when the mind peels off its not-knowing. Yet there is a sense in which the poem, for all its attestations

1. Heschel actually says that "history is devoid of poise," but he clearly means to include the current moment and thus all of time.

of multiplicity and chaos, operates from within a position of (factitious) poise, or a position in which poise is at least a possibility. The lyric instant, the form that makes the perception possible, implicitly asserts an order that the poem explicitly denies. "Snow" is a deeply spiritual poem (whatever MacNeice "believed"). One feels currents of reality usually imperceptible to us rippling through the wrought iron of its lines. But the poem is not prophetic in Heschel's sense. It takes the relationship between spirit and matter as a good, but not as a given.

Perhaps the very *need* to perceive some overarching meaning to one's life is simply one more compulsion for control, not a sign of spiritual health but of pathology, the same need to control that has decimated nature, volatilized every racial and gender relation, and locked God into holy books and human institutions. I suspect the very way I have framed this entire issue – the moment versus the flux, the sensation versus the formulation, the bright particular versus the incorrigibly plural – is itself too mired in a literary and intellectual history to admit of – much less enable – other options.

∞

I do not want a poem
that depends on madness alone
for its vision, nor on madness
alone for its madness.

Having made my meaning,
I make my meaning
clear. It is unreal
like the wings of ants.

—Ralph Dickey, "The Arcanum Poems"

Teasing out the difference between madness and vision can be a difficult enterprise for poets. And for prophets. And for anyone who has experienced – and lived to doubt – the presence of God.

Dickey's poem is a statement *about* the moment of madness or vision rather than the thing itself. It's the equivalent of criticism, or theology, or any ex post facto attempt at understanding revelation. And yet there it sits, looking for all the world like a poem, and with a glinting gem of obliquity at its heart which itself cries out for critical explanation. If you've made your meaning, why the need to make it clear? Oh, and: *unreal / like the wings of ants?*

In fact, some species of ants *do* have wings, though they appear only during the reproductive stage when an ant is seeking a mate. I feel sure Dickey was in possession of this knowledge. Might his poem be saying, then (and I do think it's the poem speaking, not the poet's idea encoded within it), that meaning is real only when it is reproduced – only, that is, when it makes its way from one mind to another? "How little and how impotent a piece of the world is any man alone?" asks John Donne. When I think of the consciousness that generates the circular sorrow of "Ifs eternally," or the one trying to find the one thing that will unify all the disparate experiences of one life, I think of a man – almost always a man, though there are notable exceptions – sitting alone in a room and doggedly trying to *figure it all out*. I read Dickey's poem as a way out of that. It is two minds that make meaning, which is an action, not a fact, or is at least catalyzed by relation, however rooted it may be in one brain. "For where two or three are gathered together in my name," Jesus promised, "there am I in the midst of them." A poem is a place where two or three can gather, and a place where revelation and explanation are not separate from each other.

∞

RALPH DICKEY DIED OF SUICIDE at the age of twenty-eight. A poem may be a locus for spiritual connection and comfort, but it's not sufficient. Let us not pretend time is not howling outside, even now, nor that the walls we make, even these, will long withstand it.

∞

CAN THERE EVER BE RECONCILEMENT between the confusion of self and the vision of truth? Between the chaos of our days and the glimpses of order and love upon which we stake our faith? Between the *If* and the *Is*?

LOVE SONG

First came cancer of the liver, then came the man
leaping from bed to floor and crawling around
on all fours, shouting: "Leave me alone, all of you,
just leave me be," such was his pain without
    remission.
Then came death and, in that zero hour, the shirt
    missing
a button.
I'll sew it on, I promise,
but wait, let me cry first.

"Ah," said Martha and Mary, "if You had been here,
our brother would not have died." "Wait," said Jesus,
"let me cry first."
So it's okay to cry? I can cry too?
If they asked me now about life's joy,
I would only have the memory of a tiny flower.
Or maybe more, I'm very sad today:
what I say, I unsay. But God's Word
is the truth. That's why this song has the name it has.

—Adélia Prado

"Let me cry first" is not in fact what Jesus said at the death of Lazarus. He didn't say anything at all in the moment of that particular verse, which is famous for being the shortest verse in the Bible: "Jesus wept." The least words for the largest sorrow. It's hardly a paradox.

What is a paradox, though, is that Jesus weeps even though he knows what is going to happen: he will raise Lazarus from the dead. His knowledge spares him nothing. It's almost as if "what is going to happen" is *contingent* upon human grief, as if fact had to pass through feeling in order to be fact.

That the fact here is a miracle only intensifies the strangeness.

We know how, in psychological terms, time can get stuck in the mind and life of someone who has not learned to properly grieve. The scene with Jesus suggests that time itself becomes sclerotic without proper sorrow. What is "proper sorrow"? "I'll sew it on, I promise, / but wait, let me cry first." Or: "If they asked me now about life's joy / I would have only the memory of a tiny flower." The loose button on the shirt of a dying man, the memory of a tiny flower in the face of annihilating pain – the details scald with irony and irrelevance. And then they burn with love. The poem is not saying that the button and the flower and grief and God's love are "related" to each other. It's saying they *are* each other. In the terms of this essay, the *if* is the resurrection this poem implies ("God's Word is the truth"). The *is* is the button. The *if* is what any honest faith looks like in this life. The *is* is the memory of a tiny flower. And they are all, for anyone fortunate enough to feel it, inseparable.

There is something both accidental and necessary, both salvaged and given, about these details and the vision of life that emerges from the poem. A whole new relation to reality seems possible. The Biblical scholar Walter Brueggemann says that what true prophetic witness enables is just such genuine newness. (This is what distinguishes such witness from the head-beating-on-the-wall method of Chekhov.) We don't want newness, though, not really. "It puts us next to the 'therefore' of God," as Brueggemann says, which might cost us our comforts and achievements, our treasured despairs. It might cost us, us. "Nothing but grief could permit newness. Only a poem could bring the grief to notice." Both true. Both ambiguous gifts of God. And *that's* why Prado's poem – and this essay – have the names they have. ⟞

Excerpted from Christian Wiman, *Zero at the Bone* (Farrar, Straus and Giroux, December 2023). Copyright © 2023 by Christian Wiman. All rights reserved.

NORMAN WIRZBA

Architecture for Humans

*Can people live in hope if their homes and places of work
do not nurture and celebrate life?*

The Butaro District Hospital, Burera District, Rwanda.

I N THE CONCLUDING LINES of "The Hell of Treblinka," one of the first published essays on the Nazi death camps, Vasily Grossman writes that lovers of humanity must always bear a simple truth in mind: "It is possible to demonstrate with nothing more than a pencil that any large construction company with experience in the use of reinforced concrete can, in the course of six months and with a properly organized labor force, construct more than enough chambers to gas the entire population of the earth." Construction workers didn't need much time to build a factory of death. They didn't need much space either: "Ten small chambers – hardly enough space, if properly furnished, to stable a hundred horses – ten such chambers turned out to be enough to kill three million people."

The architectures of terror, dehumanization, and killing were remarkably easy to build. Several of the characteristics prized by modern technocratic reasoning – precise calculation and control, maximization of yield, and machine efficiency – were put to work in the camps' design, construction, and operation. Surveying them, Grossman was struck by how much the layout and the buildings followed the principles of any large-scale modern industrial enterprise.

It is tempting to dismiss Treblinka as an especially egregious manifestation of the architecture of hell. We shouldn't. Grossman was a war correspondent for the Russian army newspaper *Red Star*. He traveled across much of Europe to report on the living conditions of millions. He saw that the brutality he observed in Treblinka was not confined to the death camps, nor was it a complete aberration. It was the logical extension of decades-old principles and policies that had the support of captains of industry and political elites. He knew that the fascism gripping Europe had not appeared out of nowhere. When Viktor Pavlovich Shtrum, one of the main characters in Grossman's 1952 novel *Stalingrad*, asks, "Who has turned the whole of Europe into a huge concentration camp?" Grossman is making a philosophical point: a morbidly sick culture creates built environments that degrade life. When people are consigned to live and work in farms, apartments, cities, mines, and factories that alienate and brutalize the soul, the sickness becomes endemic.

When thinking about forms of degradation it is important to understand that violence is not only an event but can become a material structure. A spirit of violence becomes built into the geography itself – in the qualities of neighborhoods and workplaces, and in the prevalence or lack of

healthcare, educational facilities, transportation, sanitation, and electricity. Built environments perpetuate lifestyles and practices that either frustrate or cherish life, that keep people apart or bring them together. What we build in the world communicates what we think of the world, and what we value about its inhabitants.

Consider just some of the defining material structures of the modern world:

reservations that confine indigenous peoples to undesirable land

the privatization and enclosure of agricultural land traditionally held in common

"sacrifice zones" where mining companies leave their toxic waste

massive hydroelectric projects that displace indigenous communities and alter ecosystems

mountaintop removal mining that flattens peaks and fills creeks with debris

vast fields of monoculture agriculture that depend on toxic herbicides and synthetic fertilizers to maximize commodity production

the large confinement animal feeding operations (CAFOs) that mistreat livestock and pollute surrounding watersheds

"cancer alleys" where people live on land or along waterways polluted by toxic industrial chemicals

public housing projects that consign residents to inhumane living conditions

massive slums in the world's growing megacities that lack the infrastructure to meet the basic needs of residents

the many "camps" – work camps, death camps, POW camps, internment camps, refugee resettlement camps – constructed in response to war, political persecution, and climate instability

---

Norman Wirzba teaches at Duke Divinity School. His books include Agrarian Spirit, Living the Sabbath, From Nature to Creation, Food and Faith, *and* Making Peace with the Land.

These sites are not accidental, nor are they located on the periphery. They are foundational structures upon which the modern world has been built and which it continues to develop.

THIS GRIM GEOGRAPHY alerts us to the fact that the young people of our time are inheriting built environments with considerably diminished fertility, biodiversity, and health. They are being asked to imagine their futures in a world that is increasingly polluted, ugly, and uninviting, while living in built environments poorly designed to facilitate flourishing.

Can people live in hope if their homes and places of work do not nurture and celebrate life?

In *The Timeless Way of Building*, architect and builder Christopher Alexander, along with a team of colleagues, set out to distill the design principles that have proven to promote the flourishing of communities. The team wanted first to identify built environments that promoted maximal "aliveness," and to delineate the material and philosophical elements that bring such environments into being. Their starting premise, as Alexander puts it, is simple: "We can come alive only to the extent the buildings and towns we live in are alive." The states of alienation, ennui, and despair that Alexander saw in modern societies, and the sorry state of their surroundings, convinced him that too few people appreciate the close connection between architecture and human well-being. "In a world which is healthy, whole, alive, and self-maintaining, people themselves can be alive and self-creating. In a world which is unwhole and self-destroying, people cannot be alive: they will inevitably themselves be self-destroying, and miserable."

But "aliveness" is not the same as existence – it is possible to "exist" while being "dead" to one's neighbors and neighborhood. Aliveness can be calm or stormy, tidy or spontaneous. Among its defining features, however, are the freedom and serenity that arise from the absence of inner conflict or contradiction. People who are deeply alive are at peace with themselves and their neighbors. They are at rest and feel contentment, even while being active or while struggling from time to time. They are not driven by the need to assert or impose themselves on others, or to secure their worth by acquiring more and more space. They are happy to be in the presence of others without controlling them, since the exercise of control invariably distorts and diminishes others. To be alive is to be a member of a relational whole in which one participates, in a place where one belongs.

If such people have a distinct way of perceiving and engaging their world, it follows that they will also build differently. Rather than simply imposing a design, they will first take the time to listen and be attentive to a place, assess its potential, and then work with it in ways that offer avenues for its inhabitants to express themselves. The key is to ask what this place could become if the conditions were right for its optimal growth and development, and how its design might participate in the flows and processes of life already at work. Alexander describes this as humanity's participation in the natural unfolding of things.

Alexander believes that such a commitment has long been assumed and put to work by many cultures: historically people have constructed implements and rooms, houses and workshops, neighborhoods and villages that express their understanding of themselves in the world. A home or neighborhood is a place where work and play, individual and social time, security and daring, shelter and openness come together. "When you build a thing," Alexander writes, "you cannot merely build that thing in isolation, but must also repair the world around it, and within it, so that the larger world at that one place becomes more coherent, and more whole; and the thing which you make takes its place in the web of nature, as you make it."

RWANDA MIGHT SEEM AN UNLIKELY place to see a hopeful architecture put to work. A lush country in the Great Rift Valley of Central Africa, Rwanda is remembered by many as the site of the 1994 genocide in which over half a million Tutsis were killed by Hutu militias. Rwanda's economy was severely affected by the bloodshed. Much of the infrastructure subsistence farmers needed to maintain their living was destroyed. But Rwanda is being reborn. Reductions in poverty and mortality have been profound. Biodiversity is increasing and cities now boast public gardens, genocide memorials, and clean streets.

One of the country's most beautiful and inspiring buildings is in Butaro, a small village in a remote and underserved region. Here, atop a hill overlooking rich agricultural lands, sits a hospital that was designed to cultivate the dignity of persons and celebrate the beauty of the region. Dr. Agnes Binagwaho, a former national minister of health and currently the vice chancellor of

Rwanda's University of Global Health Equity, is quoted in the book *Justice Is Beauty* as saying, "When we look at the hospital, we cannot help but admire its beauty. And the structure itself is as beautiful as the mission it embraces. It is a deeper beauty that provides everyone with what they deserve as human beings. A beauty that makes us better. A beauty that draws out of us the best things within and inspires us to give our best."

Upon entering the hospital grounds, one is immediately struck by the lush vegetation, flower gardens, and the centering presence of a large *umuvumu* tree. This tree, which serves as a traditional gathering place in Rwandan culture, communicates that this is a hospital in which people are meant to find solace, support, and companionship. The vegetation isn't simply decorative – it is well known that green spaces reduce stress and pain perception in patients. Patients and their families are encouraged to spend time outside because fresh air reduces the spread of airborne disease. This is why paths, benches, and

Construction of the Butaro District Hospital.

covered informal sitting areas dot the grounds.

The buildings are not ornate. Simple yet elegant lines communicate flow. White walls inside and out create a bright atmosphere that contrasts beautifully with the locally sourced wood trim and the volcanic rocks that have been fitted together like so many intricate jigsaw puzzle pieces. Numerous large windows look out onto pastoral scenes in the valley below, while corridors surround the perimeters to heighten the sense of sociability. When patients come to this hospital they are to feel and know through the architecture that they are surrounded by the healing powers of community and nature.

As Binagwaho understands it, beautiful architecture is not optional, an occasional ornament to alleviate ugliness:

> When we put people in an ugly, uninspiring place, we are conveying that they deserve something less than the best. . . . When we put people in a beautiful environment – and one that they had a voice in creating – then it is only natural that we will create a community which is ready to cultivate solidarity and equity. . . . We know that the environment has an impact on health outcomes and believe that if we are not able to improve the places where we work, then it will be difficult to improve the way we work.

Michael Murphy, one of the architects enlisted to design the hospital, elaborates further:

> The work and toil and maintenance that creates beauty produces a profound sense of worth. Human dignity, that feeling that we matter, that someone has noticed me for who I am, is found in those processes of beautification, the tending of the garden, the discovery that a building's design locates us in a place, that we are respected for who we are.

It is not obvious that this hospital should be beautiful. Many healthcare facilities in Africa are poorly designed and cheaply built. Rooms and hallways are grim, often patterned on the nineteenth-century European sanitoria built to isolate patients from one another. And the problem isn't simply a lack of funding that results in unclean, unlovely, underequipped, and understaffed facilities; it goes deeper, to the heart of the architectural design process itself. When Binagwaho selected the architects who would work on this hospital, she chose young architects (a design group that would eventually coalesce

---

> "The structure [of the hospital] itself is as beautiful as the mission it embraces. It is a deeper beauty that provides everyone with what they deserve as human beings."
> *Dr. Agnes Binagwaho*

---

to become the Model of Architecture Serving Society, or MASS) who would not be beholden to established conventions, processes, and forms. Murphy was part of this group, as was his former Harvard classmate Alan Ricks. What they did not realize at first was that their training at Harvard University's Graduate School of Design did not prepare them adequately for this sort of undertaking. Like many schools of architectural design, Harvard emphasizes schematic design, the creation of construction documents, building plans, and contract administration. As Ricks later observed, there was little in this education that spoke of community health, community needs, or the ability of a community to contribute to the building of its own structures.

The first attempt to design the hospital was a failure. The design didn't grow out of or celebrate Butaro and its people. It consisted of elements

chosen from a standardized list of building options that were then to be imposed on the selected location. But Murphy and Ricks realized they would need to move to Butaro, get to know the region and the people, and get local people engaged and invested in the hospital's design and construction. The mental shift required was profound: they needed to resist a scarcity mindset that assumed there would not be enough money, labor, equipment, supplies, and time to complete the project. "Perhaps the most fundamental shift," says Ricks, "was to change our preconceptions about resource limitation, and instead to look at the opportunities that abound when you are present and proximate, rather than airdropping in a prefabricated solution."

Officials from every level of government, along with thousands of area residents, were involved in the construction of the hospital. Thousands of jobs were created as people dug foundations, erected walls, laid stonework, built furniture,

added trim, and established the gardens and walkways. Once the hospital was built, hundreds more jobs were created to keep the facility going. Eighty-five percent of building costs were invested in the local economy. The people who were going to be served by the hospital also had a direct say in how it was to look and feel, with several places for people to gather comfortably and with lots of natural light and fresh air movement inside the buildings. The 64,000-square-foot facility houses 150 beds (each looking out onto the Rwandan countryside), inpatient and outpatient services, a laboratory, maternity care facilities, operating rooms, and a neonatal ICU. It continues to evolve as the people who use and administer it see where improvements can be made.

When people come to the hospital, they do not simply enter a beautiful and well-equipped facility. They see and touch buildings that reflect back to them the love, creativity, skill, and devotion that they, family members, and friends have invested

Walkways and gardens connect the buildings of the Butaro District Hospital.

in the construction. They see a place that has been created out of friendship and that honors the place and its people. They take pride in the fact that so many women and young people learned the skills of design and construction on the job there, and now have taken those skills to start their own businesses. There is a deep sense of ownership by the community because the community was involved from the beginning.

Binagwaho understood from the start that this project "must involve the people we are serving in shaping their own future. Every stone on this campus represents the work done by this community to build a better future." They also take pride in the garden that sits at the center of the hospital and that celebrates the vegetation of the region. As the master gardener, Jean-Baptiste Maniragaba, sees it, "the garden is essential to the building. When the building is finished, there must be a garden to make it beautiful. The trees bring fresh air, the flowers are beautiful. Some of them are medicinal, some are pollen-rich for bees to make honey, some have a nice odor, and they each bring out the best in the landscape. And that makes me happy. Beauty brings joy to life." When he works in the gardens and engages people he meets, he regularly exclaims, "*Nziza cyane*," which variously translates as "very good," "something is making you happy," or simply "healing landscape."

The hospital at Butaro demonstrates clearly that a building can honor a place and its community members. Too often architecture has put financial profits for some ahead of the health of a place and its people. The result has been environments and structures that are ugly, dangerous, and soul-destroying, the kinds of places that instill hopelessness. The unnecessary and avoidable creation of hopelessness should concern us because, as social justice activist Bryan Stevenson has wisely noted, "Hopelessness is the enemy of justice." As Butaro also shows, justice is created as

people focus on designing and building hospitals, schools, homes, parks, transportation networks, and places of work that enable people to feel more fully alive, more deeply appreciated and cherished.

The impulse to honor life through architectural design is growing. To give another example, across the world architects and planners are designing "twenty-minute neighborhoods" or "fifteen-minute neighborhoods" that put people in closer, walking proximity to each other and the various amenities – shops, schools, eateries, healthcare facilities, green spaces, recreational parks, community centers, and entertainment venues – that facilitate a humane life. People have grown tired of sprawling, car-dependent spaces that segregate life's functions and leave people feeling isolated and alone. They are asking for housing and public places that maximize personal encounters and promote better physical and mental health.

Such neighborhoods are at their best when area residents come together to decide what will best facilitate mutual flourishing. Following what is often called asset-based community development (ABCD), the goal is to build environments that facilitate quality relationships, in which people get to know each other and become a source of mutual help. Public benches, parks, and squares are often prominent because they encourage people to linger and spend time with each other. One of the clearest signs of a vibrant and healthy neighborhood is that people of all ages – with their strollers, bicycles, wheelchairs, and walkers – are found safely and comfortably moving within them.

A hopeful architecture communicates that people and places are cherished. By reflecting loving intention in their design and construction, neighborhoods and buildings can make the people who work and play and rest in them feel valued. We need more architecture like this. ➤

Hunger

In this story set in 1990s Armenia,
survivors of war find a reason to go on living.

NARINE ABGARYAN

Translated from the Russian by
Margarit Ordukhanyan and Zara Torlone

NEMETSANTS ALEKSAN lingers in the cellar to feast his eyes on the fruits of his daily labor: the broad-necked clay pots, whose aroma gives away their contents even with the lids closed: this one has pickled cabbage, the ones over there have marinated beets, chervil, and purslane, all nestled up next to homemade cheese of every variety – fatty *brynza*, mildly brined *chanakh*, stringy *chechil*, ripe sheep's milk cheese with herbs. Through the dark glass of their pot-bellied jars, honey and clarified butter emit an incandescent glow. The big storage bin is tightly packed with bags small and large containing various sorts of flour, dried fruit, nuts, and grain;

the smaller bin, with peas, beans, and wheat. The ceiling is hung with smoked meats: ham dressed in a thin layer of fat, links of homemade sausage, fiery-hot pork-belly roulade trussed snugly with twine. The shelves are crowded with jars of winter preserves: fruit jams and jellies, compotes, stewed meat, baked and stewed vegetables. The potato pit is filled to the brim with choice tubers layered with dried river sand; carrots, beets, and cabbage lie packed in wooden boxes with ventilation holes to keep the vegetables fresh. Clusters of grapes and husks of dried corn hang from the sturdy beams; apples and pears sit waiting for their designated hour; persimmons, sun-colored and sweet, are slowly ripening; quince glisten, buttery-yellow underneath their delicate fuzz. Watermelons, lined up in a row, rest against the wall with their striped sides, daydreaming of summer.

Nemetsants Aleksan and his wife, Arpenik, have a big farmstead: two orchards, a vegetable garden, a chicken coop, an apiary thirty beehives strong, a rabbit hutch, a barn big enough to house three cows and eight sheep, and a pigpen. While Aleksan is out breaking his back over the harvest, his wife takes care of the house and the animals: she does all the washing, cleaning, and feeding, and takes the cattle out to pasture. From dawn till dusk, she bustles about in the kitchen, baking, frying, sautéing, boiling. Making winter preserves is painstakingly hard; *ghaurma* alone takes so much effort – first, the meat has to be braised with spices over low heat for almost twenty-four hours (to the point of fainting, Arpenik likes to joke), then it has to be packed into jars with scalding hot butter and canned immediately before it cools. The canned meat goes a long way in the lean winter months – just fry it up with eggs or add it to any soup or porridge. Aleksan lends his wife a hand whenever he can steal a moment

from his own work: he'll fire-roast the eggplant-tomatoes-peppers here, purée the raspberries with sugar for jam there, or grind the roasted wheat into *pokhindz* (a course flour used for porridge, *khavits*, in the winter) in the stone mill – Arpenik doesn't trust the new electric grinders and prefers to use the old intractable contraption she has inherited from her great-grandmother. Arpenik is reluctant to accept her husband's help and keeps trying to convince him to take a quick nap instead – get some sleep and give your arm a little rest. He obliges, but after tossing and turning for a few minutes, goes back to her. She shakes her head disapprovingly but doesn't say anything. What *can* she say – at their age, insomnia is the norm.

They send some of what they make to their adoptive daughter, leave a small portion for themselves, and sell most of it at the farmers' market where the townsfolk go to stock up on market days. Aleksan is unfailingly polite and patient with them; townsfolk are like kids – they know nothing about fruits and vegetables and can't even tell *salceson* from ham. He explains, in detail, which apples to buy for now and which for storing, expounds on how and with what to eat the cured meats, offering samples that he cuts not in little translucent slices but in generous big pieces. Some of the customers gratefully accept his advice, others politely cut him off – thanks, we'll figure it out. He never insists – my job is to explain, the rest is up to you. Some of the customers are so unpleasant that he wonders how the earth carries them – condescending and rude, they buy from him as if doing him a favor. He treats the fact of their existence with resignation: say what you will, every herd has a bad sheep. What good would it do to get worked up over something you can't change?

Born in Berd, Armenia, Narine Abgaryan is the author of a dozen books including Three Apples Fell From the Sky *(Oneworld, 2020).* Plough *will be publishing her story collection* To Go On Living, *from which this story is taken, in 2025.*

Ask Aleksan what his biggest fear is, and he'll answer without hesitation: hunger. Pain can be soothed with medicine, cold can be spooked off with warmth, fear can be chatted away. But nothing can placate or cheat hunger; it hovers overhead in a cloud of infernal darkness, taunting you and killing every shred of your humanity. Aleksan is intimately acquainted with hunger; he lived with it for two endlessly long years, for twenty-five terrifying months: the winter when, never imagining that Berd would soon be under siege, people carelessly cleaned out their winter preserves and found themselves with nothing to eat in February; the spring when they were bombed during peak sowing season, preventing people from working in the fields; the summer when the entire sky was blanketed by smoke from the torched wheat fields; the fall when they couldn't even make it to the forest to forage for wild fruits; the winter when a tiny trickle of aid – grain, powdered milk and eggs, and tea – finally started getting through the mountain pass that was under constant enemy shelling, so that at least the kids could hold out until the arrival of warmer weather, while the grown-ups, and especially the elderly, departed one after the other; you'd wake up in the morning to find Grandma dead already, and Grandpa would be barely breathing and gone by sunset; the following spring when, desperate enough to ignore the enemy fire, the people went out into the fields to till, and not everybody came back – some were cut down by bullets, others taken hostage, but there was no other alternative: war or hunger, it was all the same death; the summer when hail the size of human fists destroyed everything, literally everything, except the potatoes, which the people hoped would last them till spring; the fall when the harvest began disappearing from fields and orchards, and they all suspected each other at first until they discovered that it was the townspeople; it turned out they were starving too, but didn't know how to live off the land, so they were stealing from the villagers. Aleksan found this upsetting but he couldn't help pitying the townsfolk: How could you hold a grudge against people who had been driven by despair over the treacherous mountain pass to scavenge food for their families by theft?

"Nothing can be more frightening than hunger," thought Aleksan, and he knew exactly what he was saying because he had stared hunger straight in the face. It had come to him in the guise of an emaciated old man with sunken cheeks, a thread-thin line of bloodless lips, and papery skin stretched taut over his sharply protruding cheekbones. "If you weren't careful, you could cut yourself running your finger over them," randomly flashed through Aleksan's mind. It was as if the old man could sense his thoughts; his translucent eyelids, under which a slight move-ment of his dark pupils was detectable, flickered, but he couldn't muster the strength to open them. He was lying on his side, his neck awkwardly twisted and his left arm splayed on the other side, his chin pointing up, and faint traces left by dried tears ran from the outer corners of his eyes toward his temples; in a senselessly repetitive motion, he kept clawing at handfuls of frozen soil with his right hand; his pants had slid down, revealing his sunken stomach and the flabby funnel of his belly button; his leg had turned black and was bleeding where the trap had snapped around it, crushing the bone to a pulp. He was silent the entire way as Aleksan drove him to the hospital, and only grimaced slightly when the car hit potholes. As he was being moved to a gurney, he clutched Alek-san's hand and pulled him down. Aleksan, leaning over to make out the words through the old man's raspy, labored breathing, went pale, and then mouthed: "Just give me the address, I will handle the rest." The old man mustered the strength to tell him the address.

From the hospital, Aleksan headed straight to Musheghants Tsolak's house. Tsolak was out back, chopping wood. When he saw his guest, he set

down the ax and went to greet him, ready with a smile and a handshake. Aleksan made a tight fist and punched him once, then a second time right in his smiling lips. Dodging a return blow, he ducked and, without taking his eyes off Tsolak's face, felt for a log. Wincing from the pain that shot through his crippled left arm, Aleksan clobbered Tsolak in the stomach with all his might. Tsolak went down with a sob. Aleksan stood over him for a bit, waiting for his rage to subside, then spat and rubbed his saliva into the ground with his boot. Then he plopped down and helped Tsolak turn over onto his back.

"Why did you set a bear trap on your plot?" demanded Aleksan, still short of breath and stuttering. "What were you hoping to catch? A jackal?"

"What trap?"

"Don't play dumb," Aleksan spat out angrily.

"Who got caught in the trap?"

"An old man. A refugee."

"So if he is a refugee, then it's fine for him to steal?" Tsolak sat up, swung around with unexpected adroitness, and slapped Aleksan across the face. Aleksan neither dodged the blow nor tried to return it. He swallowed, feeling the unpleasant taste of his own blood.

"He's definitely going to lose his leg. That's if he pulls through. He has a great-granddaughter in town and nobody else. He lost everyone else in the pogroms."

Tsolak got up, picked up the log that Aleksan had used to clobber him, and tossed it back into the mound of chopped firewood without looking. The log landed at the very top, got caught on another log by a chipped piece of bark, and hung suspended in the air.

"So my kids aren't kids, then?" he hissed in a whisper. "Half of my relatives are not refugees, right? It's OK to steal from me, right? Because I'm a pansy and not a man, right? And I don't have a right to eat!"

Aleksan also got up and dusted off his pants.

"Anyway, I'm off. You are in charge of the old man."

"Off where?"

"To get his great-granddaughter from town. He says she hasn't eaten for five days."

It was a long ride to town, four hours over a road torn and gutted by shelling. The town struck Aleksan as oppressive; it looked exactly like the border villages – just as deserted, forlorn, and steeped in gloomy darkness and cold. Every house, every street, every window exuded desperation and loneliness. He had no trouble finding the old man's apartment in a dank neighborhood on the outskirts of the city, on the first floor of a ten-story cement construction, whose windows, down to the last one, were hung with blankets on the inside in a desperate effort to preserve whatever scant warmth there was. The girl's eyes, as it turned out, were of two different colors: one green, the other hazel. Aleksan's great-grandmother would have called it the devil's mark, which he made sometimes so that people wouldn't forget about his presence. Aleksan offered the girl a handful of dried prunes, which she accepted after some hesitation, and not before thanking him. She ate slowly, with dignity. When she was finished, Aleksan told her to pack all of their belongings, hers and her great-grandfather's, and she complied without complaining or asking questions. They made it back to Berd around midnight. They raced through the mountain pass so fast they risked missing a turn or plummeting off a cliff, but there was no other way – car headlights make excellent targets for sharpshooters. Mercifully, they made it home without incident.

The old man passed away that very same night – his heart couldn't take it. Aleksan buried him next to his own parents. The girl cried all the time, didn't answer any of their questions, was afraid of darkness and closed doors, and screamed if someone shut the door to her room. It took a while for Aleksan to figure out what it was she feared, but it finally occurred to him to take the door off the hinges, and she calmed down at once. Her name was Anna, and she was twelve, although she looked barely nine: small, frail, quiet. She ate very little, tried not to leave the house if she could avoid it, and if she went outside, she didn't go past the yard. Once, she wrapped her arms around Aleksan and told him, in a terrifying whisper, that once upon a time everything used to be wonderful in her life, that both of her grandparents were schoolteachers in Baku, that her father built houses while her mother raised her younger brother, but how one day they were all gone because some people stormed into their apartment and killed everyone except Anna – at the last moment, her grandmother had shoved her underneath the sofa and told her to stay put no matter what, but she didn't have time to also hide her four-year-old grandson, and Anna saw how someone's dirty boot tripped him as he was trying to run away, how he fell, banged his face against the floor, and started crying, and how the same dirty boots landed full force on his back, jumping on it until the boy stopped moving. Her great-grandfather smuggled Anna out of Baku in a suitcase – he made holes in the sides to make sure she didn't suffocate before making his way through the pogrom-engulfed city. Before shutting the suitcase lid, he asked for her forgiveness in case they both got killed.

"But we didn't get killed, as you can see," she concluded, raising her wondrous varicolored eyes to Aleksan. "Please don't be mad at him, he used to be a scientist and didn't know anything other than his science. When we got here, he found a job as a night guard, but they were holding back his pay. Nobody would lend us money because we were refugees. We had to make rent for the room because the landlady kept threatening to kick us out, I kept crying all the time because I really wanted to eat,

and my great-grandpa put up with it for as long as he could. Then he said he couldn't stand to see my tears and went to find us some food."

Ask Aleksan what the purpose of human life is, and he'll say without hesitation: caring for others. For relatives, for loved ones, for all the ones who remain. Of all his kids, only the youngest survived the war. Now he lives in faraway America and

---

Ask Aleksan what the purpose of human life is, and he'll say without hesitation: caring for others. For relatives, for loved ones, for all the ones who remain.

---

only visits once in a while. He keeps asking his parents to go live with him, but they won't budge – the graves of our forebears are here, and this is where we will lie as well. Anna has long moved to the big city and become a journalist; now she travels all over the world writing clever articles. Everyone seems to have found a place in life, so Aleksan and his wife can finally breathe a sigh of relief and live for themselves. But there is also Yepime, the sunshine girl, the daughter of Aleksan's sister who died in childbirth. Aleksan and Arpenik visit her every Sunday, both to see how she's doing and to remind her of them – she's got a bird-like memory and only recognizes people whom she sees regularly. When the time comes, they will have her come live with them. Life has meaning for as long as you have someone to take care of, Aleksan likes to say. Arpenik doesn't disagree – what's the point of arguing if he is completely right: life only has meaning if you have someone to live for. ➤

Daniel Bonnell, *Annunciation*, mixed media on grocery bag paper, 2004

Yielding to God

The Christ Child is born in the poverty of our hearts.

PHILIP BRITTS

WHEN THE WISE MEN, or the kings, came from the East, they went to Jerusalem, the capital, to inquire, "Where is he who has been born King of the Jews?" And today those who are "wise" make the same mistake in looking to worldly power to solve the world's problems. Others go to magnificent cathedrals and follow spiritual paths that appear much more splendid and much more clever than anything which accompanied the birth of Christ.

All this is misguided; it concentrates on the question of "how" instead of the question "why." We can easily get overwhelmed. How are we to carry out all the tasks laid upon us; how are we to plan our next year; how shall we find the strength both for securing our economic needs and for reaching out to the needs of others? But as important as these questions are, it is more important to remember the ancient question "Why?" Once we realize why Christ came to earth, why he was born as a helpless baby in a manger, and why his whole life was lived as an outcast from the best society, then can we begin to answer the question "how"–how can we find God again; how can we experience peace on earth?

We are human and finite, and thus cannot live perpetually in a sense of expectation, or in a continuous Advent. We are distracted by many things. Our spiritual awareness waxes and wanes in intensity. If an attitude of expectancy, or an inclination to poignant spiritual experiences, is cultivated by conscious effort of our own, we will suffer severe limitations. Such effort totally misses the mark. We may get lifted up in moments of tenderness but will be cast down in hours of dryness. The swing of emotions is natural to us, and some

---

Philip Britts was a British poet, farmer, and member of the Bruderhof. During World War II he moved to Paraguay, where he died of a tropical illness at thirty-one. This selection is from an address given on December 12, 1948, and appears in Watch for the Light: Readings for Advent and Christmas. *See page 118.*

Daniel Bonnell, *Mary and her Baby*, oil on canvas, 2004

are more subject to extremes than others. We mustn't despair about this. But we should be aware of cultivating religious emotions under the delusion that these are the workings of the Holy Spirit. Such emotions are unstable; they risk getting in the way of our communion with God.

It is here that we need to see why it was necessary for Christ to come to the earth. God has come to us because we, by our own power of soul, by our own emotions, even the noblest and most sublime,

can never attain redemption, can never regain communion with God.

True expectancy, the waiting that is genuine and from the heart, is brought about by the coming of the Holy Spirit, by God coming to us, and not by our own devices. Spiritual depth, if it is true, is the working of God coming down and penetrating to the depths of our hearts, and not of our own soul's climbing. No ladder of mysticism can ever meet, or find, or possess God. Faith is a power given to us. It is never simply our ability or strength of will to believe. The spiritual experience that is truly genuine is given to us by God in the coming of his Spirit, and only as we surrender our whole lives to an active expression of his will.

To put it quite simply, spiritual experience, whether it be of faith, hope (or expectancy), or love, is something we cannot manufacture, but which we can only receive. If we direct our lives to seeking it for ourselves we shall lose it, but if we lose our lives by living out the daily way of Christ we shall find it. Spiritual experience, if it is of God, will indeed lead to a life of activity. But *the nature of the true activity is surrender and obedience.* The most striking revelation of this is found in the conception and birth of Jesus. When the angel Gabriel came to Mary, he told her, "The Holy Spirit shall come upon you, and the power of the Most High shall overshadow you." And she answered, "Behold the handmaiden of the Lord; be it unto me according to your word."

It was in this submission, this surrender and obedience, that Christ was conceived. And it is the laying down of power that is revealed in his birth. Christ did not spring armed from the head of Zeus. He came as a child. He was not even born in the protection of a royal court, with soldiers to guard against intruders and physicians to guard against sickness. Rather, he was born in a stable, at the mercy of Herod and the stark elements of cold and dirt.

This pattern of complete abandonment of human strength in total surrender to God's will is of vital importance for us, both in our lives of activity and of spiritual experience. It was in the surrender of herself to God that Mary became the mother of Christ. It was in her acceptance of Gabriel's message that the great decisive event of history took place. And in our own daily lives, in our efforts to do right, what is decisive is that we accept and live by and surrender ourselves to a strength which is not our own, to the piercing white light of God's love.

When we experience this love we turn away from the notion that we initiate and God responds; that we, by our religious efforts, can set something in motion that God must obey in response. To believe that by an effort of will we can mount nearer to God or add one cubit to our stature is as unchristian as the belief that we have no task as Christians for the mundane affairs of this world. Both beliefs have the same root–the pride that seeks to climb its way to God–and produces the same kind of confusion as the ancient attempt to build the tower of Babel.

The direction to which our wills must be put is in obedience to God's will in response to the

---

It was never Christ's purpose to bring about self-improvement. He became poor not to offer us a moral toning up, however good this may be. The Word became flesh so that the same amazing life that broke into the world when Jesus Christ was born actually becomes realized in our own lives here and now.

---

breaking in of the Spirit. Then something decisive happens *for this earth.* In place of the confusion of injustice, strife, open war, and treachery, there is revealed a path of the most lively unity and clarity. And in obediently following this path we are released from the servitude of our own desires, our selfish hopes and fears–we are redeemed, we become free.

If decisive and liberating Good is to be born on this earth, it must, like in Mary, find room in humble surrender. This does not mean a passive life of inaction. Far from it. The service of God makes the most impossible demands of us, demands which we know our strength cannot carry out, or which our hearts cannot bear. But our calling is obedience, even to the hardest demands; and we must take them up in the faith that our minds or bodies will be supported by the strength of God.

Although we are tempted to exert ourselves and push ourselves forward in our search for God, the desire to climb nearer to God is nothing but egotistical satisfaction and self-aggrandizement. The way that Christ took was the low way. His way is abandonment. He not only descended from the presence of God, but he came as a baby in the poorest conditions. It is not that we, as pilgrims, climb to a celestial city, but that the Christ Child is born in the poverty of our hearts. Surrender does not mean the cessation of seeking, for we must always seek the will of God in every situation. We seek in order to obey. And in obeying the small thing that we see, the greater is revealed to us. True surrender never separates itself from carrying out God's will.

This is why we do not come to know God by musing or by contemplating our highest ideals in splendid spiritual isolation, nor by disputing religious points and striving for a state of spiritual perfection. No, God comes to us when we offer a cup of water to the thirsty, whether it be plain water in an enamel cup or the water of life found in God's Word.

But let us not be deceived by such humble gestures. Human love cannot redeem. If it could there would have been no need for God to be born as a human child on this earth.

There is something altogether different from goodwill that we need. This something was fulfilled in the coming of Christ and in the manner of his coming. This amazing difference is fulfilled in our own lives when the Christ Child is born in our hearts. This is not an abstract experience or a flush of emotions, but a concrete acceptance of his Word. The birth of Christ is an example both unique and eternal of how the will of God is worked out on this earth. It is the birth of love in our hearts, which transforms life. God's love overwhelms us and breaks into our lives, leaving our human goodwill behind. It was never Christ's purpose to bring about self-improvement. He became poor not to offer us a moral toning up, however good this may be. The Word became flesh so that the same amazing life that broke into the world when Jesus Christ was born actually becomes realized in our own lives here and now.

The meaning of Advent and Christmas is thus the coming down of God's love. This love alone revolutionizes our lives. Only God's love, not the elevation of human souls, can effect a transformation of the world. Those who mourn the futility of their own efforts receive the comfort of the love of God. Those who are meekly obedient to his will are filled by the love of God, not as a prize to be won after death, but as redeemed life for this earth.

Human love depends on human character and certain virtuous qualities. It propels some people to attain greater heights than others. A spiritual hierarchy is thus created in which each person climbs to a different height of godliness or saintliness according to his or her spiritual capacity. This is not the way of the manger. The love of God lays low all such hierarchy. Gifts, however spiritual, are not decisive. What is decisive is *agape*, the pure unconditional love of God.

Human love lifts up the Good Man. It is just this that Christ reveals as missing the point, when he himself, speaking as a man, says, "Why do you call me good? There is no one good but God." All our human goodness is relative; there is nothing in us immune from evil. Besides, Christ came not for the righteous but for sinners, for all those who can say, "Be it unto me according to your word."

The peace on earth the angels proclaimed is reconciliation with God. It is brought about by the coming of Christ into our poverty. In John's words, *"Herein is love: not that we loved God, but that he loved us."*

PLOUGH BOOKLIST

Subscribers 30% discount: use code **PQ30** at checkout.

Members 50% discount: call for code or check your members-only newsletter. Plough Members automatically get new Plough books. Learn more at *plough.com/members*.

New Releases

Tears of Gold
Portraits of Yazidi, Rohingya, and Nigerian Women
Hannah Rose Thomas

This debut art book by British artist and human rights activist Hannah Rose Thomas presents her stunning portrait paintings of Yazidi women who escaped ISIS slavery, Rohingya women who fled violence in Myanmar, and Nigerian women who survived Boko Haram captivity, alongside their own words, stories, and self-portraits. A final chapter features portraits and stories of Afghan, Ukrainian, Uyghur, and Palestinian women.

HRH The Prince Charles: I very much hope that this beautiful book will help enable these women's voices to be heard, as well as to highlight the issue of the persecution of religious and ethnic minorities in general.

Hardcover, 128 pages, ~~$49.95~~ **$34.96 with subscriber discount**

Inner Land
A Guide into the Heart of the Gospel (Complete Boxed Set, Vols. 1–5)
Eberhard Arnold

Inner Land might seem to be about the cultivation of the spiritual life, yet Eberhard Arnold writes: "The only thing that could justify withdrawing into the inner self to escape today's confusing, hectic whirl would be that fruitfulness is enriched by it. It is a question of gaining within, through unity with the eternal powers, that strength of character which is ready to be tested in the stream of the world." *Inner Land*, then, calls us not to passivity, but to action.

5 hardcover volumes in slipcase, ~~$98.00~~ **$68.60 with subscriber discount**

Called to Community
The Life Jesus Wants for His People (Second Edition)
Dietrich Bonhoeffer, Dorothy Day, Fyodor Dostoyevsky, Richard J. Foster, Jonathan Wilson-Hartgrove, Søren Kierkegaard, Chiara Lubich, and others

This book's fifty-two chapters will ignite a weekly group discussion. They are by people who have lived in intentional community and know what it takes. Whether you have just begun thinking about communal living, are already embarking on a shared life, this collection will encourage, challenge, and strengthen you.

Softcover, 406 pages, ~~$19.95~~ **$13.97 with subscriber discount**

Christmas Gifts

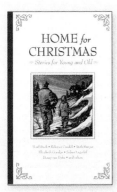

Home for Christmas
Stories for Young and Old

Pearl Buck, Rebecca Caudill, Ruth Sawyer, Elizabeth Goudge, Selma Lagerlöf, Henry van Dyke, and others

They are some of the warmest childhood memories, those unhurried evenings around the fireplace, Christmas tree, or dinner table, when there was time for a story. . . . Now, with this collection, you can keep the storytelling tradition alive in your family, and pass it on to your children or grandchildren. *Home for Christmas* includes twenty time-honored tales. Several are by world-famous authors; others are little-known treasures translated from other languages. Selected for their literary quality and spiritual integrity, they will resonate with readers of all ages, year after year. Now in a deluxe hardcover gift edition.

Jim Trelease, author, *The Read-Aloud Handbook*: If you're giving one book for Christmas, make it this one.

Hardcover, 339 pages, ~~$22.00~~ **$15.40 with subscriber discount**

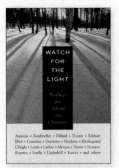

Watch for the Light
Readings for Advent and Christmas

Dorothy Day, C. S. Lewis, Oscar Romero, Philip Yancey, Dietrich Bonhoeffer, Meister Eckhart, Søren Kierkegaard, Annie Dillard, Kathleen Norris, and others

Ecumenical in scope, these fifty devotions invite the reader to contemplate the great themes of Christmas and the significance that the coming of Jesus has for each of us – not only during Advent, but every day.

***Publishers Weekly*:** These are not frivolous, feel-good Advent readings; they are deep, sometimes jarring reflections, many with a strong orientation toward social justice.

Hardcover, 344 pages, ~~$26.00~~ **$18.20 with subscriber discount**

When the Time Was Fulfilled
Christmas Meditations

Alfred Delp, Eberhard Arnold, and Christoph Friedrich Blumhardt

The forty short meditations in this collection witness to the fact that the birth of Jesus is more than history for those who feel their need of him.

Christmas is the season of joy for good reason: it is the news of a savior being born, of light breaking into darkness, of God's peace and goodwill to all. But joy is more than merriment. For those who feel bankrupt, without real meaning or hope – either for themselves or for the world – Christmas can be genuinely life-changing.

Softcover, 166 pages, ~~$10.00~~ **$7.00 with subscriber discount**

(continued from p. 120)

on at least one occasion, the Emperor Frederick Barbarossa, when he had yet again interfered in church politics. "I see you like a little boy or some madman living before the Living Eyes," she wrote, warning him to shape up and stop electing antipopes.

And, apparently, she continued to have the visions that fueled this wealth of insight and creativity. She had first seen what she called "the Shadow of the Living Light" at age three. "I have seen great wonders since I was a child," she told Bernard, and she really didn't know what to make of them. "Most gentle Father, you are secure; in your goodness please answer me, your unworthy servant, for since I was a child I have never felt secure, not for a single hour!"

She's been posthumously diagnosed, as other visionaries have, with hystero-epilepsy, with migraine (though she mentioned no head pain to go with her visions), and so on. But such diagnoses do virtually nothing to reach into the experience and mind of this remarkable woman.

What we know is what she tells Bernard, and us: she has seen visions and received teaching about them; she believes that the teaching regards spiritual readings of the scriptures, but she's worried that she may be going wrong. "I only know how to read for the simple meaning, not for any textual analysis. . . . I am taught inwardly, in my soul. Therefore I speak as one in doubt." She's something like Saint Paul going to Saint Peter to make sure that his visionary experience of Christ lines up with the concrete historical teachings of Christ. She wants to lay her understanding at the feet of the apostles, to not go haring off after esoterica.

Her entreaty itself gives a flavor of the way reality presented itself to her – or rather the way God presented himself to her, and presented the cosmos as his creation. "I entreat you: by the brightness of the Father, by his wonderful Word, by the sweet humor of compunction, by the Spirit

of Truth, by the sacred sound through which all creation resounds, by the Word from which all the world was created, by the height of the Father who through the sweet power of green vigor sent the Word to the Virgin's womb where it took on flesh like honey in the honeycomb!"

She was captivated by this sense of the living reality of God's life imbuing all of the cosmos – and the microcosm of the human body – with the "green vigor" of the Spirit. And

---

"The soul humidifies the body so it does not dry out, just like the rain which soaks into the earth."
Hildegard of Bingen

---

the strength and insight that these visions gave her enabled her to help build the international body of the church, knitting it together with letters offering political, spiritual, and personal advice, and with poetry and painting and medicine and music and motherly affection.

A remarkable event marked the last year of Hildegard's life; it demonstrates her steadfastness in the face of injustice. A nobleman who had been excommunicated died after making his confession to a priest and receiving the sacraments. Hildegard had him buried in the convent cemetery. The prelates of the diocese of Mainz, claiming falsely that there had been some impropriety in the young man's reconciliation, demanded that his body be exhumed. Hildegard refused. The clergy placed her convent under an interdict, forbidding the nuns to receive the sacraments or to sing the liturgy. Hildegard, as usual, wrote letters, advocating for her nuns and herself, and several months before her death the injunction was lifted. ⌖

Susannah Black Roberts is a senior editor of Plough. *She and her husband, Alastair Roberts, split their time between New York City and the United Kingdom.*

The Sweet Power of Green Vigor

In music, art, medicine, and spiritual writings, a spunky medieval nun named Hildegard of Bingen sought to express "the sacred sound through which all creation resounds."

SUSANNAH BLACK ROBERTS

AND I, A HUMAN BEING, neither ablaze with the strength of strong lions nor learned in their exhalations, remaining in the fragility of the weaker rib, but filled with mystical inspiration, saw . . .

IN THE WINTER OF 1148, in Trier in Germany, Pope Eugenius III found himself with a manuscript, a half-finished work of a curious nature. The pope's former teacher Bernard of Clairvaux had brought it to him; Bernard had received it more than a year earlier, with a cover letter that addressed him in terms at once anxious and confident.

"Venerable Father Bernard," his interlocutor had written, "you are held in wonderfully high honor by the power of God. . . . Father, I ask you, by the living God, to attend to my questions."

The writer was a nun, the abbess of a small convent in the Rhineland. Born in 1098 to a noble family, the tenth child, she was given as a tithe to the church, and dedicated as an oblate. At some point before she was eighteen, she took the vows of a nun.

We know little of the next twenty years of her life, but in 1136, the nuns of her convent chose her as abbess. It was in 1141 that, with the encouragement of a monk called Volmar, a friend, she started to write.

She had a lot to get down.

She had had visions.

It was the content of these visions, and her reflections on them, that Pope Eugenius III found in the manuscript that his old teacher presented to him. Impressed with their strange, vivid authority and convinced of their orthodoxy – though it was an orthodoxy expressed at times in highly original terms – the pope confirmed Hildegard's visions as legitimate and gave permission for the work to be published.

Hildegard's life changed drastically after that. She spent the next thirty years as a public figure: an author, political advisor, and spiritual director. She undertook many speaking and missionary tours throughout Europe and founded two new convents. She composed music and made visionary works of art, reproductions of what she saw: pieces that look for all the world like mandalas containing detailed allegorical figures.

As well as her visionary and theological works, she wrote scientific and medical treatises, songs, and an opera, which her nuns performed. She corresponded with many of the leading figures of her day: four popes, many churchmen, and,

(continued on previous page)

About the artwork: Hildegard of Bingen is shown here in the dress of the Benedictine order. The flame and the parted curtains signify the visions she received. The stylus to one side of her symbolizes her writings and music, and to the other side her initials appear in the alphabet she created. The ring around her head reflects the mandala style of her artwork.

Opposite: Cory Mendenhall, *Hildegard of Bingen*, watercolor and ink on paper, 2023.